**Contemporary
Art Station**

Published by the Contemporary Art Station.
All artworks © 2024 Don Taylor "Plein Air Journaling in Watercolor and Pen & Ink"

ISBN: 978-84-19926-85-2
DL: GR 9-2024

Printed in Europe by Contemporary Art Station.

DON TAYLOR

PLEIN AIR JOURNALING IN WATERCOLOR AND PEN & INK

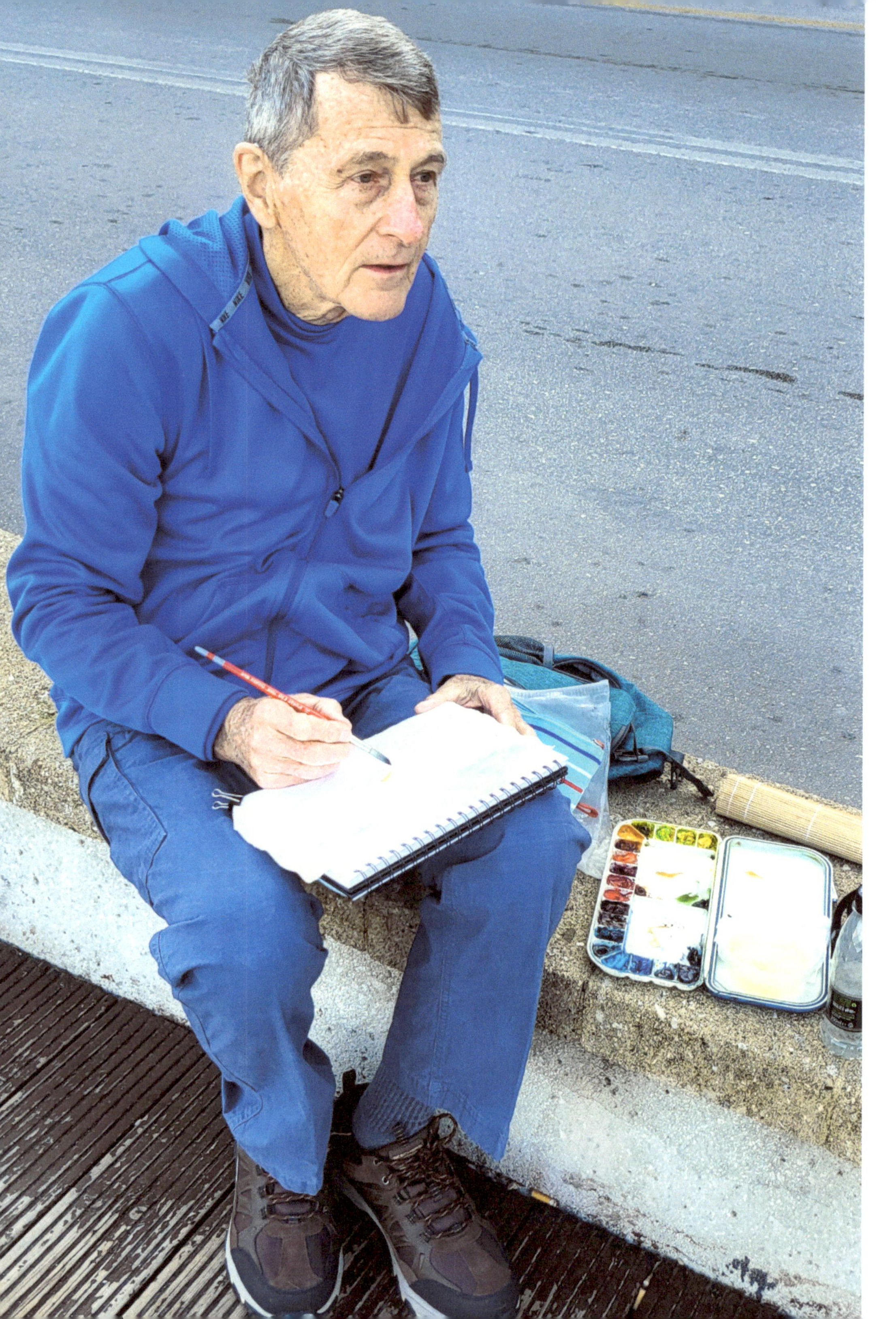

PLEIN AIR JOURNALING
IN WATERCOLOR AND PEN & INK

A brief history of how I evolved into a full time professional artist is in order. It might even encourage others that were in my situation to do the same. My father graduated from art school after high school, but instead of fine art, he took up metal crafting. From early elementary school until I graduated from high school, I worked in his shop. During that time, he always encouraged me with my artistic endeavors.

While at the University of Florida there was no time for art and I graduated in 1964. I was commissioned in the USMC and reported for 3 years of active duty. My last year was a tour of duty in Chu Lai, Viet Nam. After discharge as a Captain, I acquired a MS degree at UF and then was accepted in the Auburn School of Veterinary Medicine.

In 1972, I entered veterinary practice in Panama City, FL and still live in that area. After about 25 years of full time practice, I started part time in order to pursue my passion for watercolors. Prior to 1972, I worked in oils and acrylics, but then started taking watercolor classes in 1974. Around 2006, I began teaching classes locally and workshops regionally. In 2003, I started my travel journaling in watercolor/pen & ink and hope to continue that as long as possible.

I completely retired from veterinary practice in 2018 after Hurricane Michael ravaged our area. Over the years, I became a signature/elected member of 18 major watercolor societies.

There are two people in my life that I would like to dedicate this book to for a number of reasons. First, my wife Louisa who traveled with me on most of these trips and who usually very patiently walked with me over long distances and waited while I painted these sketches. Most spouses do not care much for the boredom of watching someone do this, but Louisa hung in there with me for most of them!

Additionally, our son, Rick has traveled with me to several locations while I'm on my painting expeditions. Our trips were always enjoyable and he has given me great pride in that he has asked me to leave him my travel journals when I am gone. I could not hope to leave them in better hands!

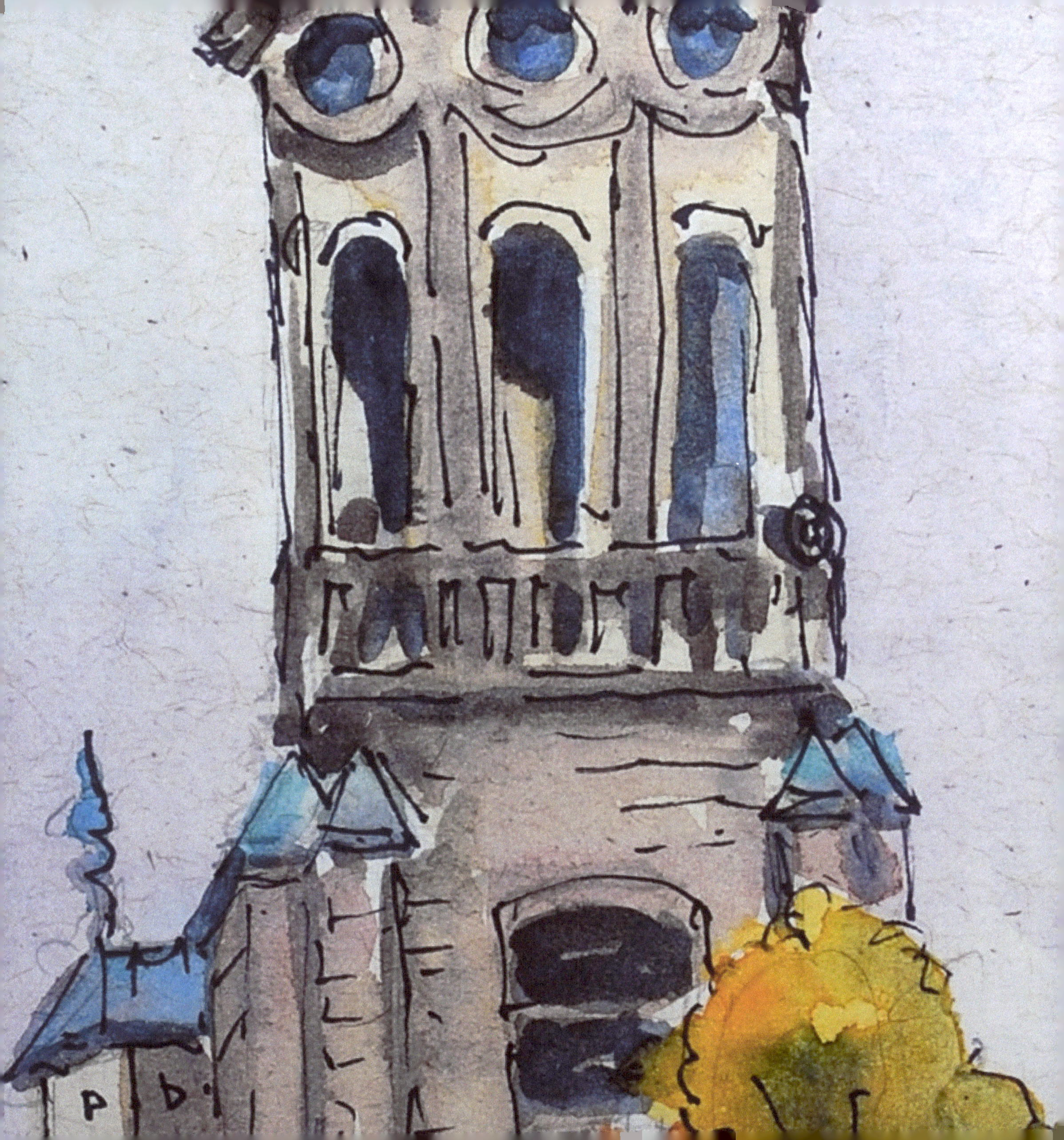

PLEIN AIR JOURNALING IN WATERCOLOR AND PEN & INK

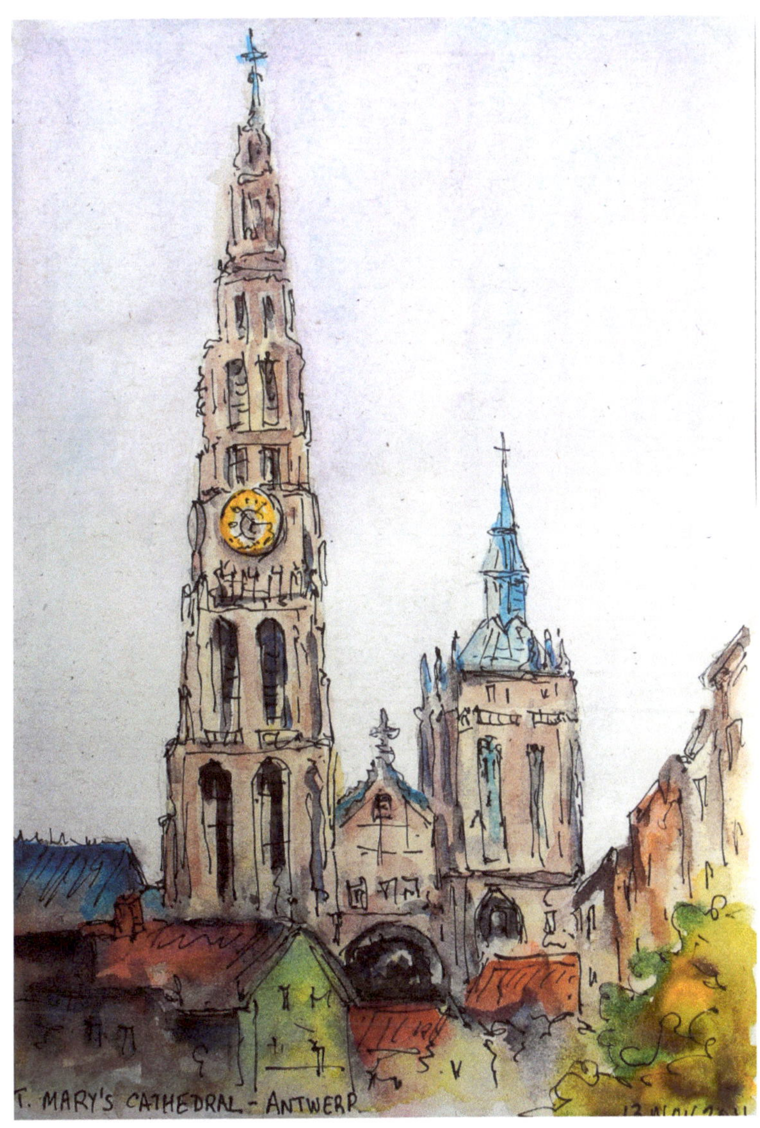

Antwerp

This sketch of St. Mary's Cathedral in Antwerp is a good example of what we may have to endure as far as the elements are concerned...the temperature was just above freezing and there was a fierce wind from the waterfront which was behind me. The wind chill factor was well below freezing. My wife had long since headed back to the river boat for a hot chocolate. My hands, feet and face were numb and I was trying to paint with gloves on! In this case, I cheated and finished the pen and ink when I got back to the boat and thawed out!

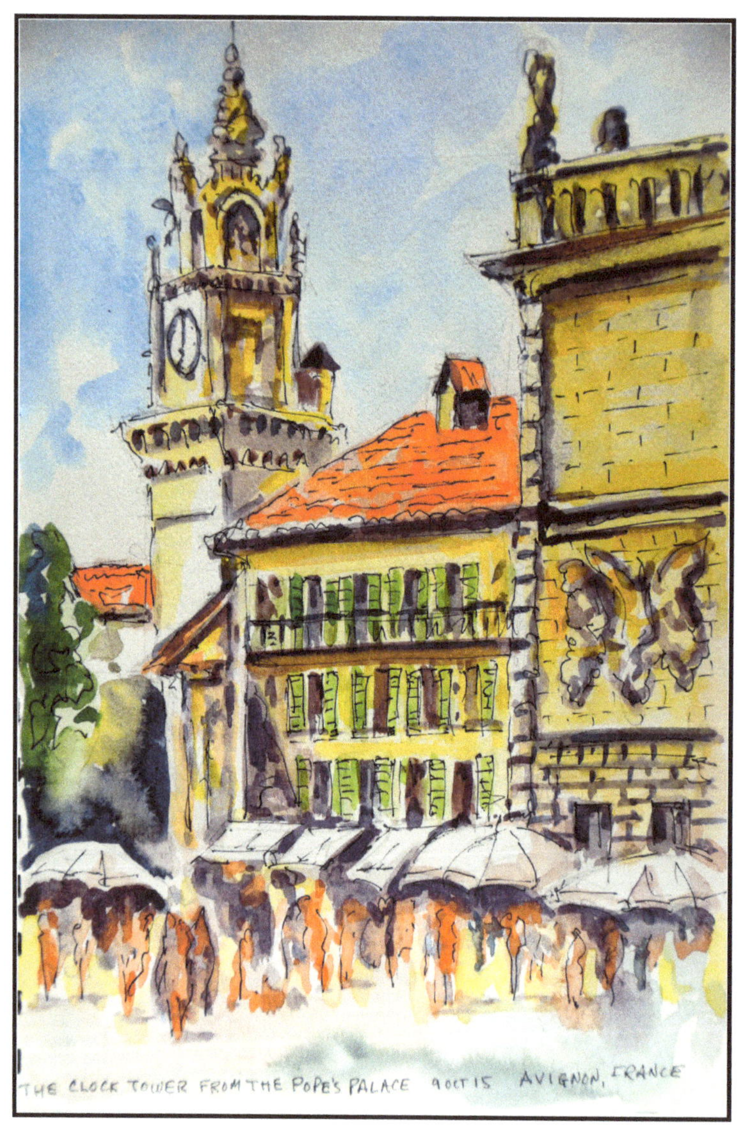

Avignon, France

Avignon is a beautiful medieval town that at one time was the residence of the Pope. There is a well preserved wall around most of the city and the preserved structures are great subjects to paint. There is a large local population that live there as well as many tourists coming through, but it's worth the visit if you're in the Provence area of France. This is a view from in front of the Pope's Palace looking toward the Clock Tower. I included this image because it shows how you can add images suggestive of large crowds of people without much detail. A busy market place just has to have people in it!

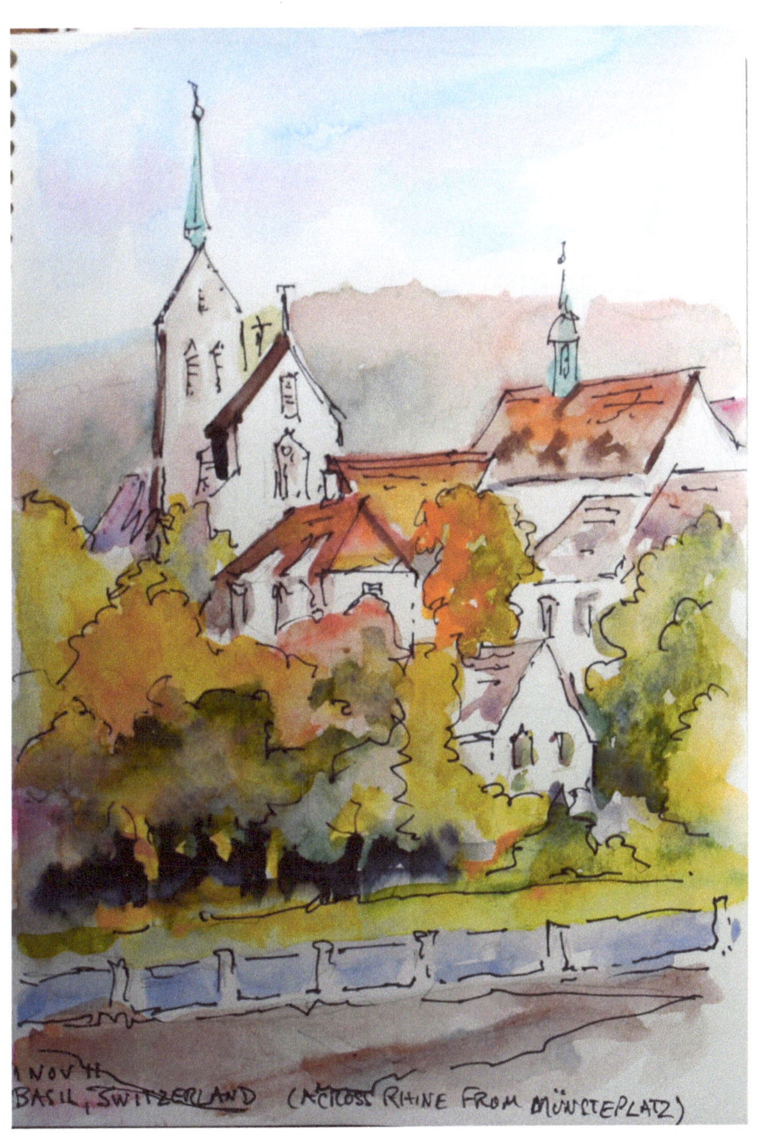

Basil, Switzerland
There were many places to paint along the various rivers connecting Basil, Switzerland and Amsterdam, but this is one that I remember the most. I was in a small courtyard of a church overlooking the river in Basil with a wonderful view of the town on the other side. It was in November, so it was beginning to get a bit chilly, but it was a sunny day and people were out in droves enjoying the sun. Later on, during the cruise, the the weather turned overcast and cold....that's where I froze in Antwerp!

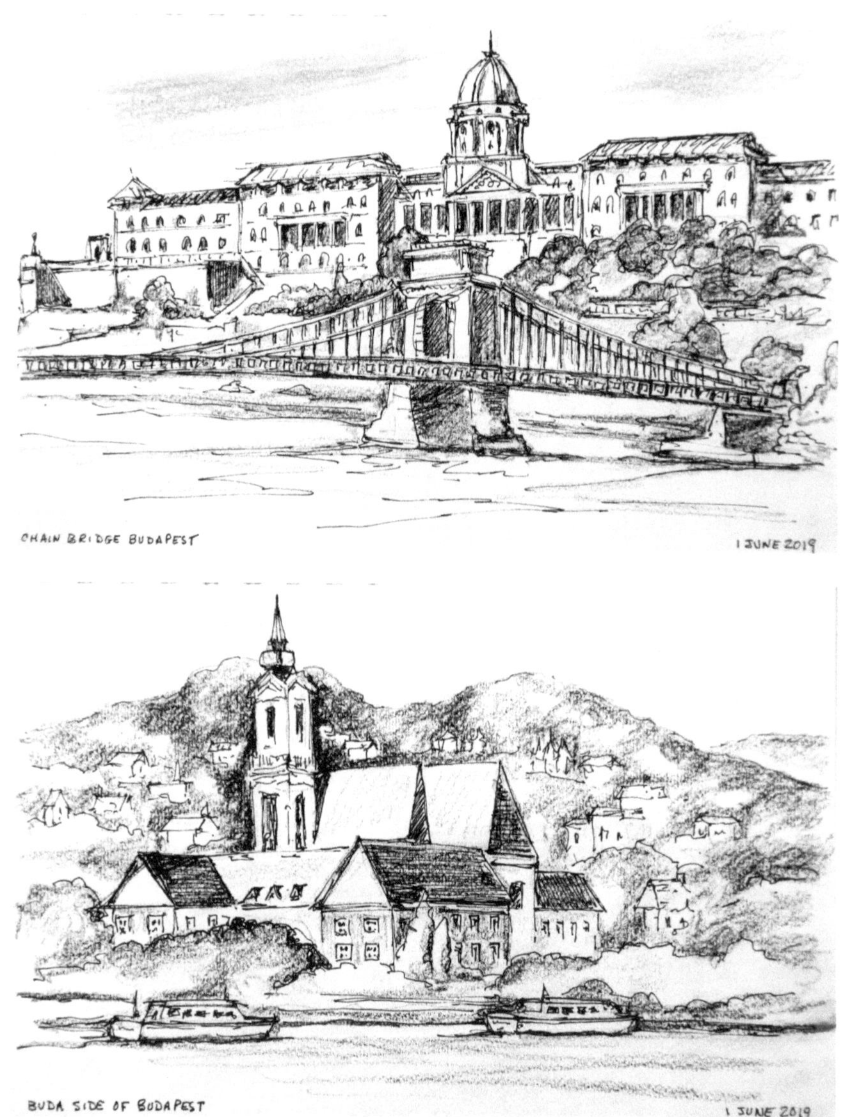

Budapest-Transylvania

During a return trip to Budapest on our way to Transylvania, we encountered one of the nightmares of traveling....losing your checked luggage for 7 days! I have always carried my journal in my carry on luggage so as to never have that out of my sight, but the rest of my paints, brushes, etc. were in my checked luggage. In this case, I found an artist's pencil and just did pencil drawings for 7 days. Here are two of those drawings. You might notice that the Chain Bridge is the same view as the earlier watercolor sketch from several years prior. This is just another example of how you must maintain flexibility in adverse situations!

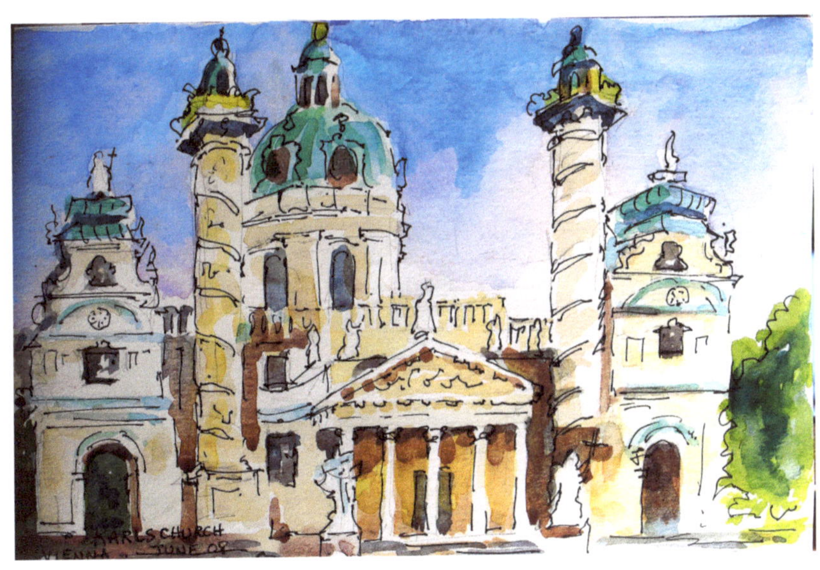

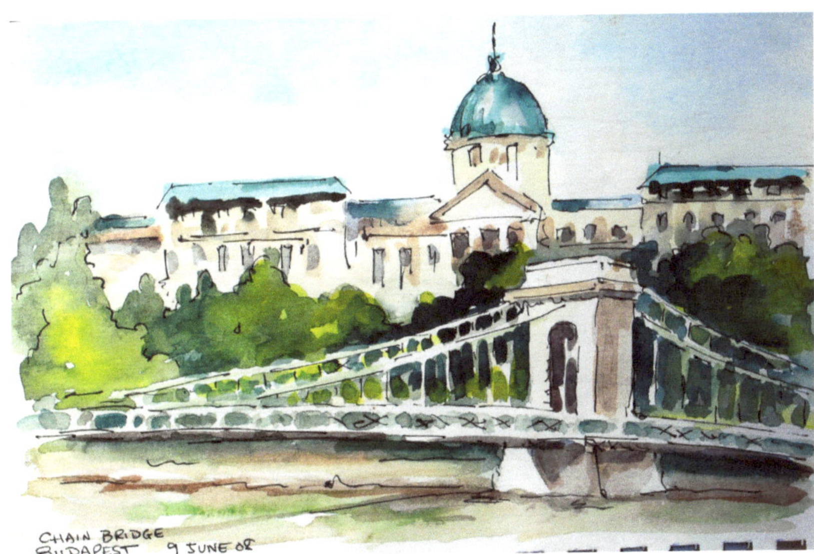

Budapest

We spent time in Budapest while on a Danube cruise and I wandered around the city until I found a view of the Chain Bridge from the other side of the river with the Houses of Parliament in the background. This created a perfect angle.   I used the trees in the middle ground to highlight the bridge by using negative painting. In my plein air journaling, I try, when possible, to establish my center of interest utilizing the Golden Mean.

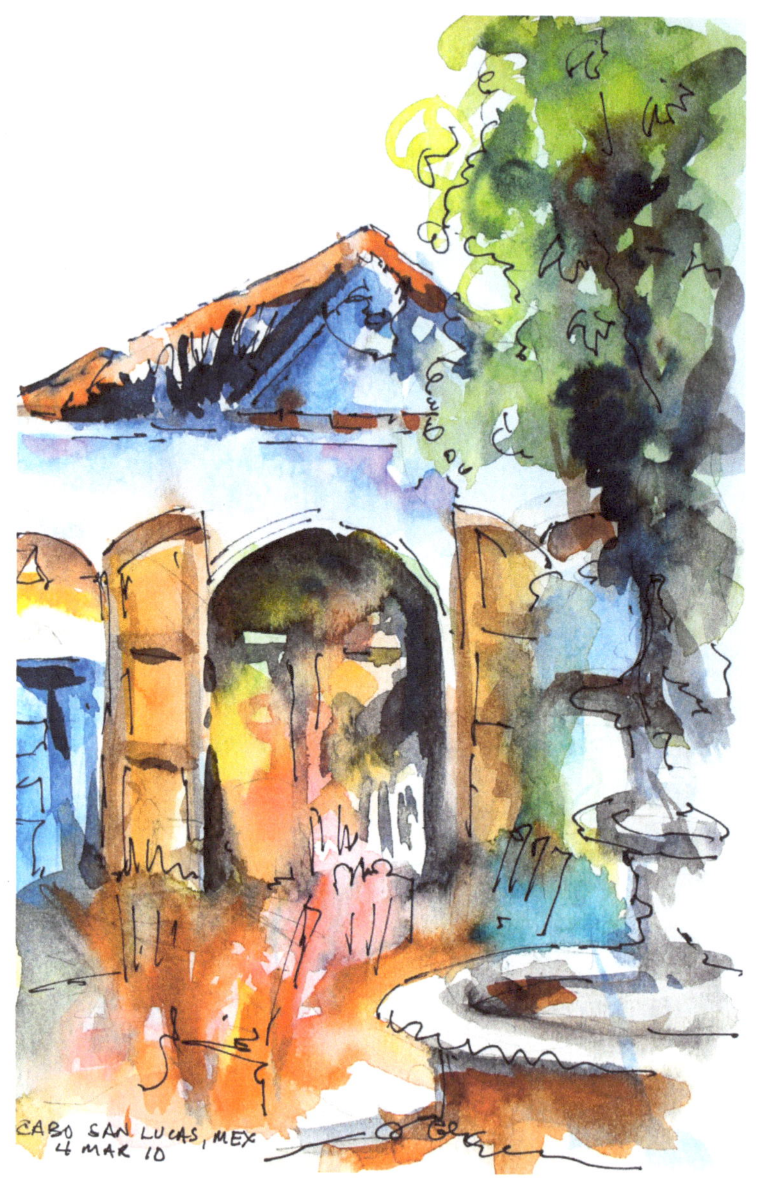

Cabo San Lucas
This very quick sketch was done in Cabo San Lucas, Mexico. My wife and I were on a cruise that stopped there and we wandered through the small town. It was hot and we decided to stop in a tapas bar and have a beer. Out on the back patio, we had a beautiful fountain and foliage, so I did a sketch while sipping a Corona with lime!

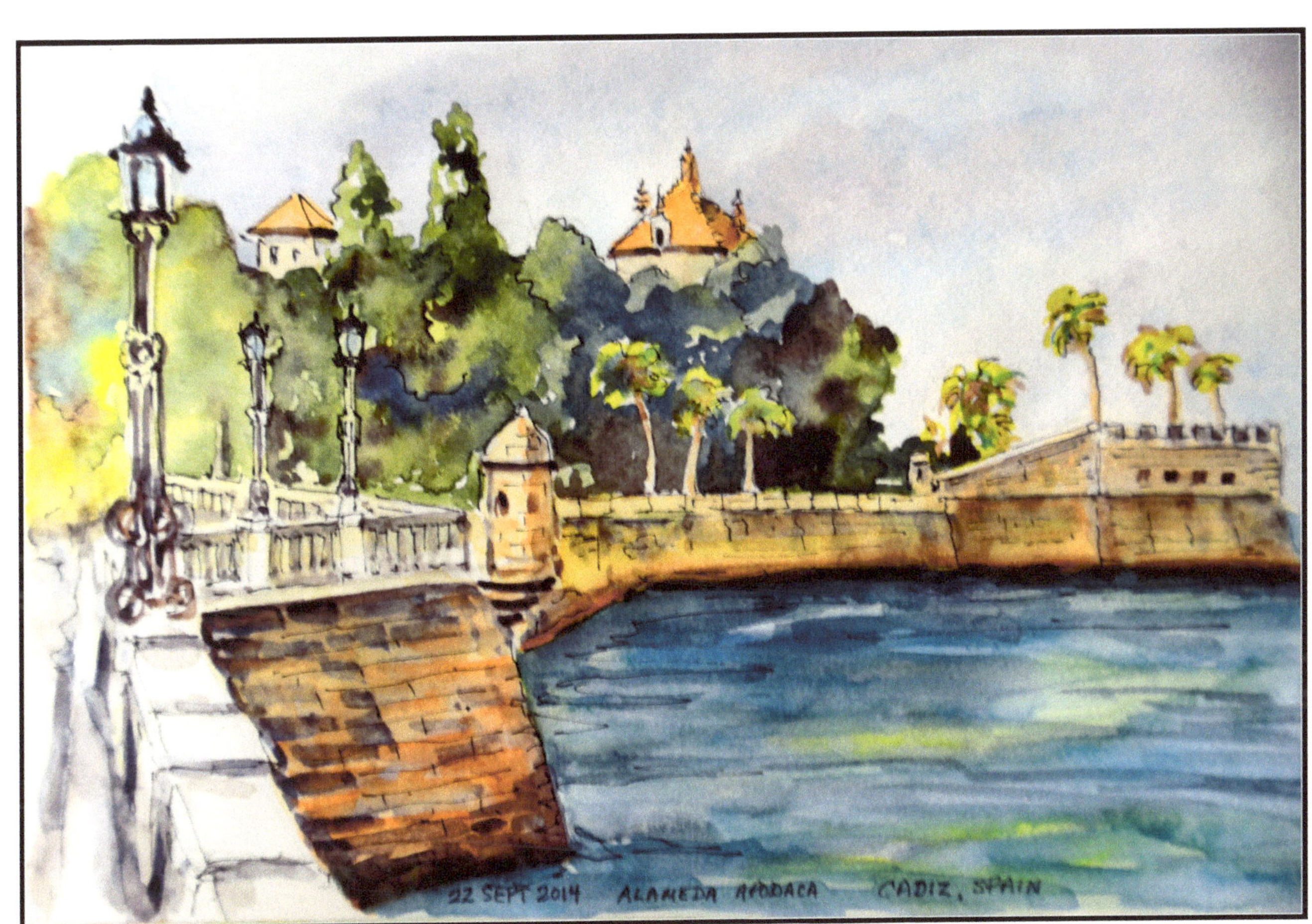

Cadiz, Spain

Cadiz, Spain had many scenic views, but the best ones I found were waterfront scenes. The architecture was interesting, but you could follow the road from the harbor along the bay and find lots of great places. This is one view along the road following the shoreline with the hills and houses in the background. This provided a natural path for the viewer's eye to follow. Water scenes ate actually much easier and quicker to do than complex architectural scenes.

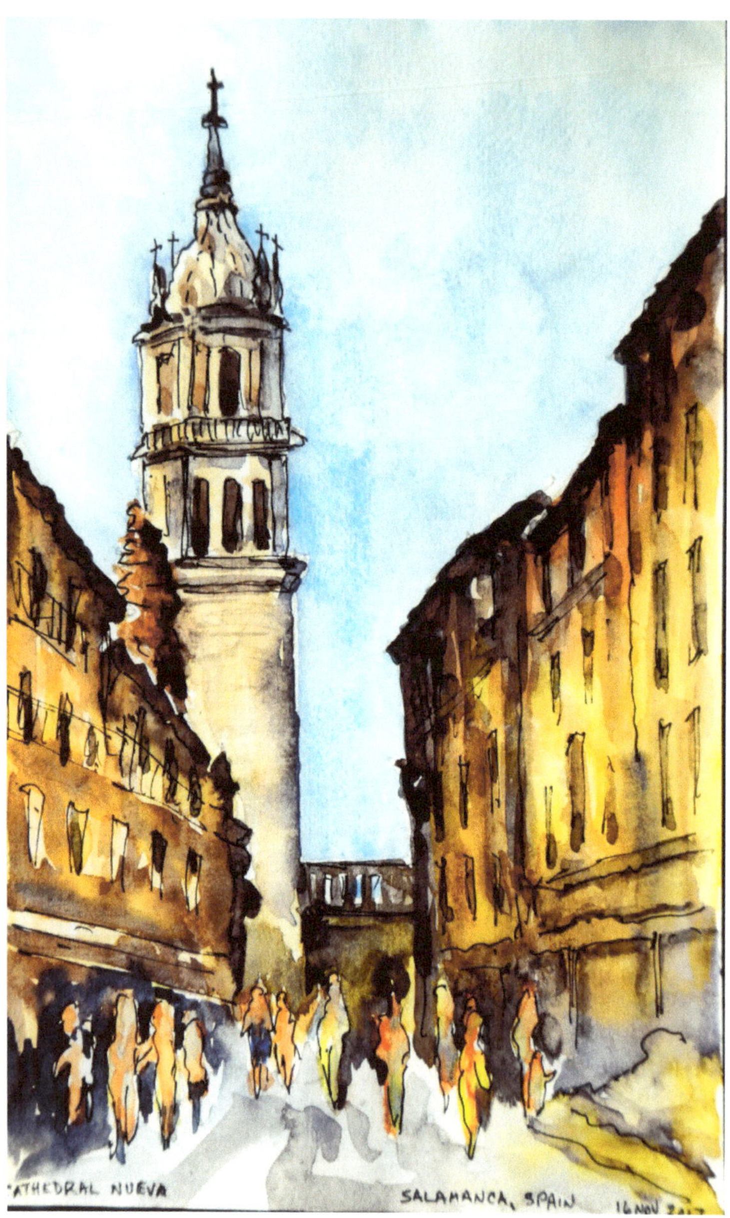

Salamanca, Spain
On a side excursion from a Douro River trip, we went to Salamanca, Spain. Salamanca has a beautiful old city within the original walls, with a very old university, cathedral and other fantastic architectural gems. The cathedral at some time in the past was damaged and had to be rebuilt, hence the name Cathedral Nuevo. This view has the cathedral in the distance, with the street taking you to it's base. I've done two studio paintings of the interior of the cathedral, which has beautiful natural lighting and acoustics.

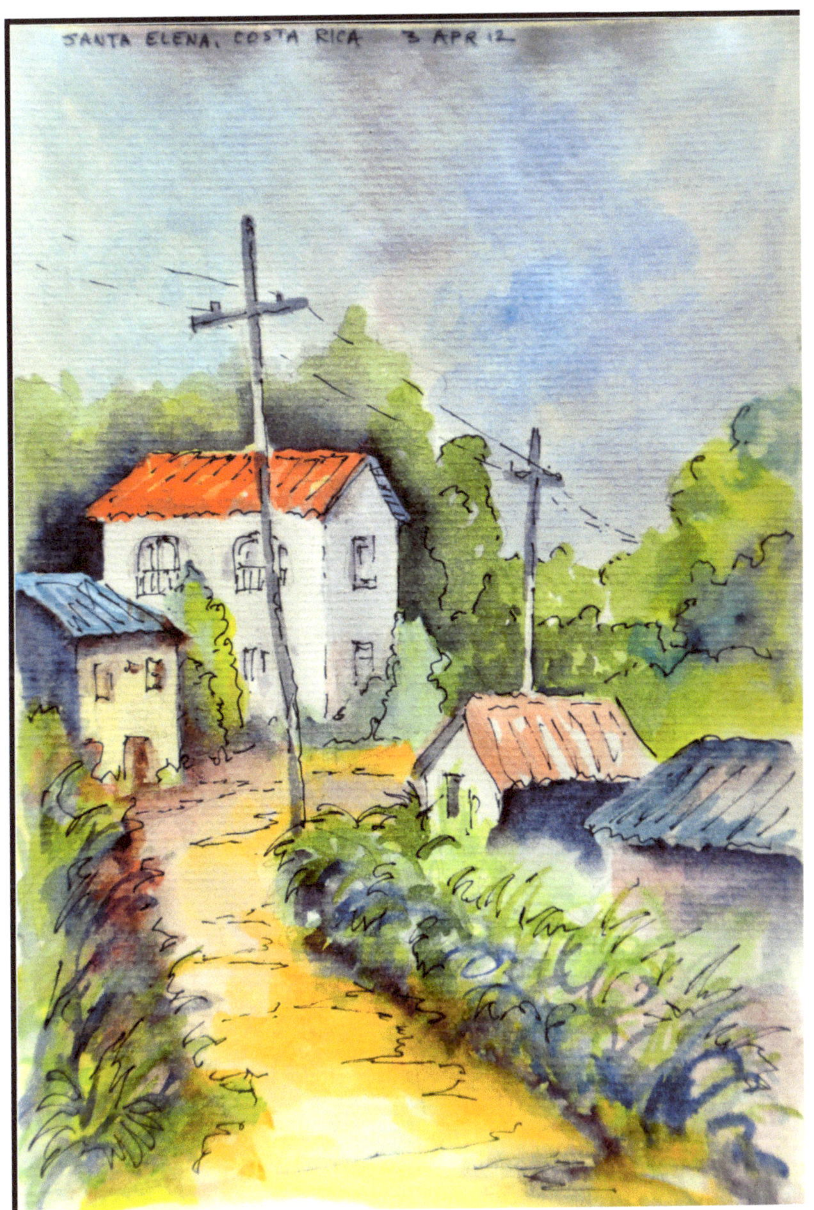

Santa Elena, Costa Rica
On a trip to Costa Rica, we had a bunch of free time, so I did a lot of wandering around looking for scenes to paint. This painting was done on a dirt trail in a small community called Santa Elena, accessible by foot, 4 wheel drive, or donkey. I liked it because of it's simplicity and trail leading to the center of interest. It's a reminder to not overlook something that may seem too mundane to paint!

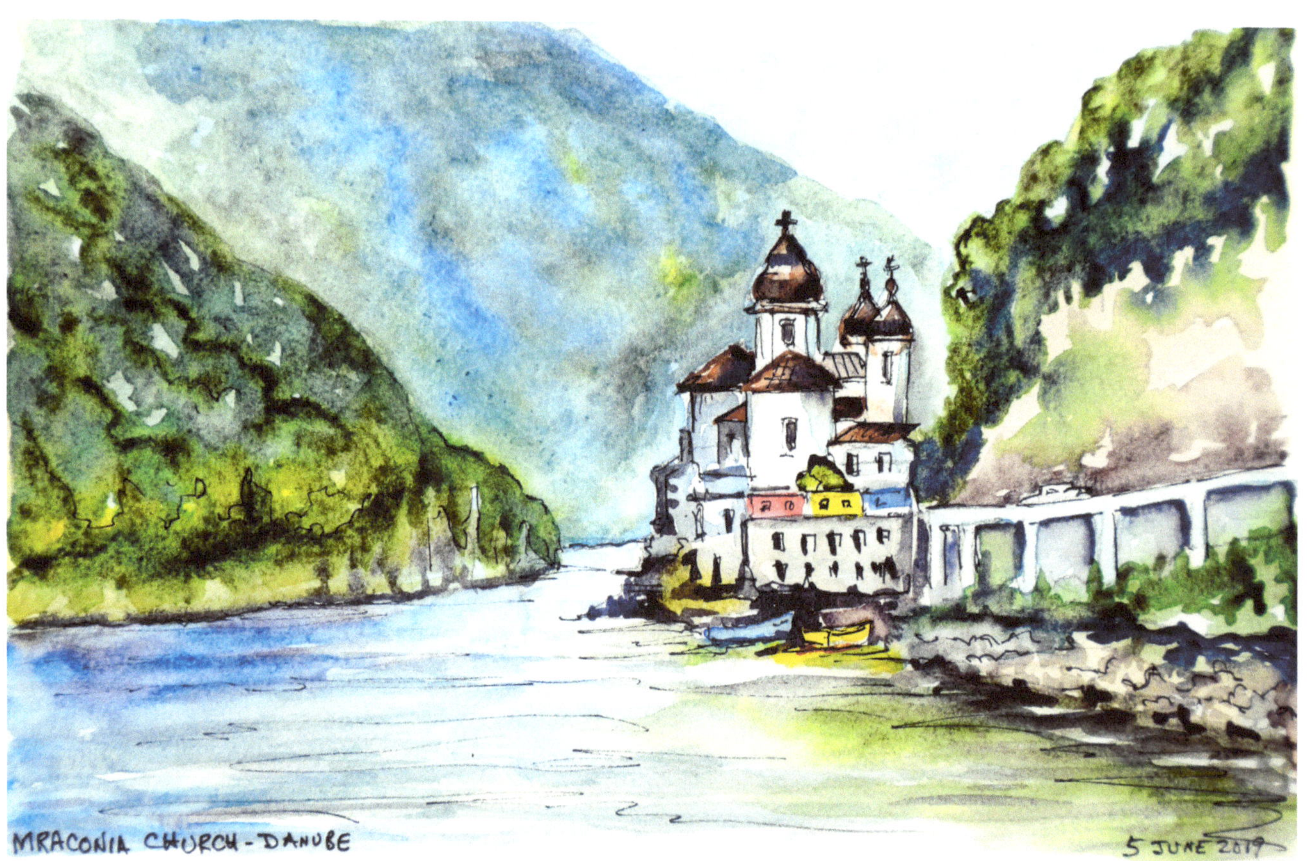

Mraconia Church, Danube
This scene from along the Danube is a fine example of how you sometimes have to work with a moving target, so to speak. Our river boat was moving slowly through one of the narrow areas of the river and this was one of the most scenic spots we had seen. I had to work fast to get my basic drawing and paint on the paper and then do some of the detail and ink touches from memory since the boat had moved on. Remember, adapt is the key word!

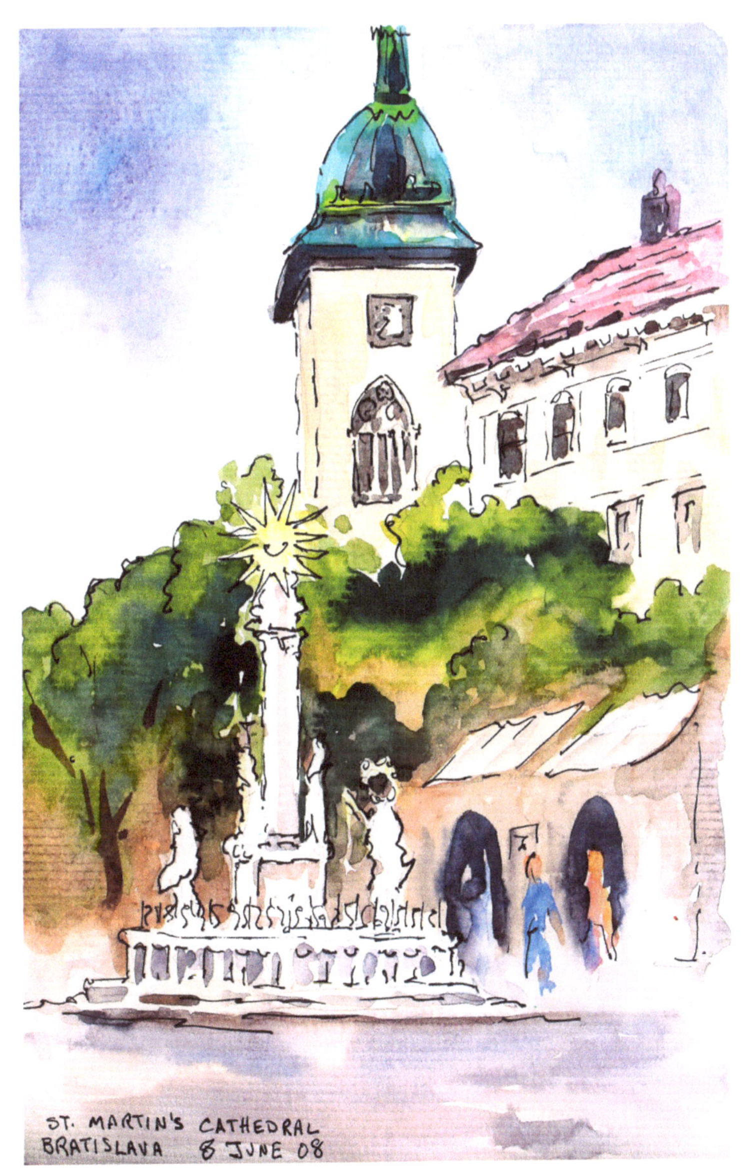

St. Martin's Cathedral, Bratislava

Another stop along the Danube in Bratislava provided a nice composition with St. Martin's Cathedral in the background and a monument/fountain in the foreground. The trees and foliage in the middle ground provided a good backdrop for the fountain. I used the white of the paper for the fountain and painted around it to bring out the shapes. Adding some people to the sketch brings life to the painting!

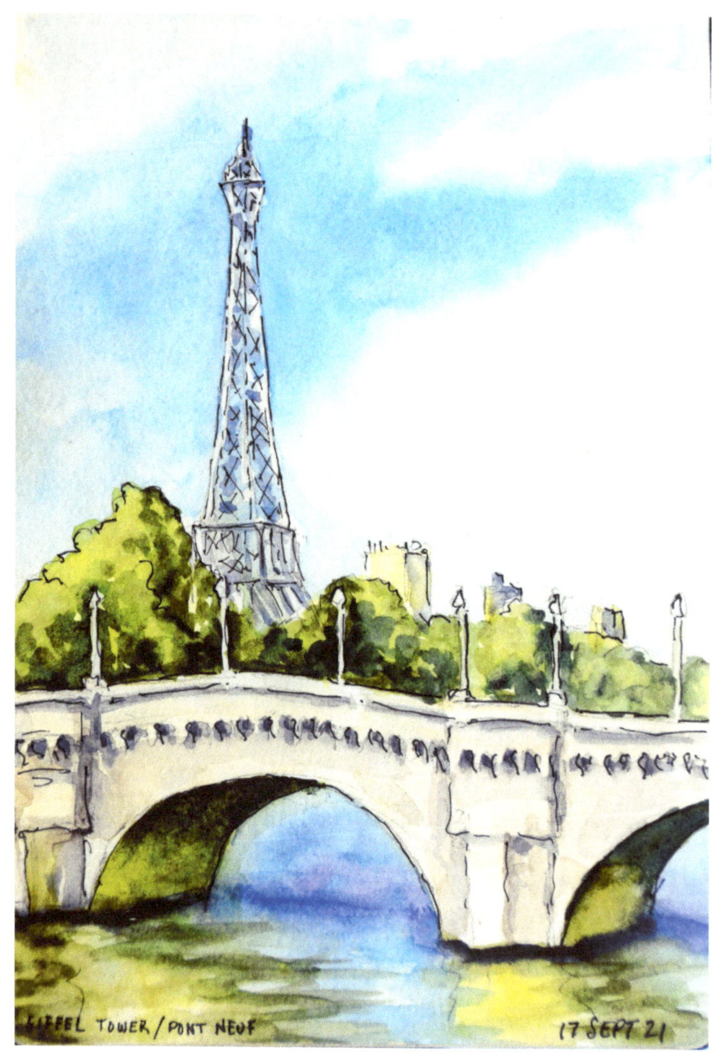

Eiffel Tower, Paris.
In Sept, 2021, I spent a week in Paris, roaming the streets and looking for painting subjects. My tiny apartment was conveniently located and I had wonderful sunny weather, except for rain the morning I arrived and the morning I left! Of course, Paris is a painter's dream that everyone needs to visit! It's not really a huge city, and easy to navigate on foot.
The first image is of the Eiffel Tower with the Pont Neuf in the foreground. It was a lovely Sunday and all the locals were out walking, cycling or jogging that morning.   While I was working on the sketch, I had numerous locals stop and comment on my work. All of them thought I was a local also, but that wasn't a problem as art is truly universal!

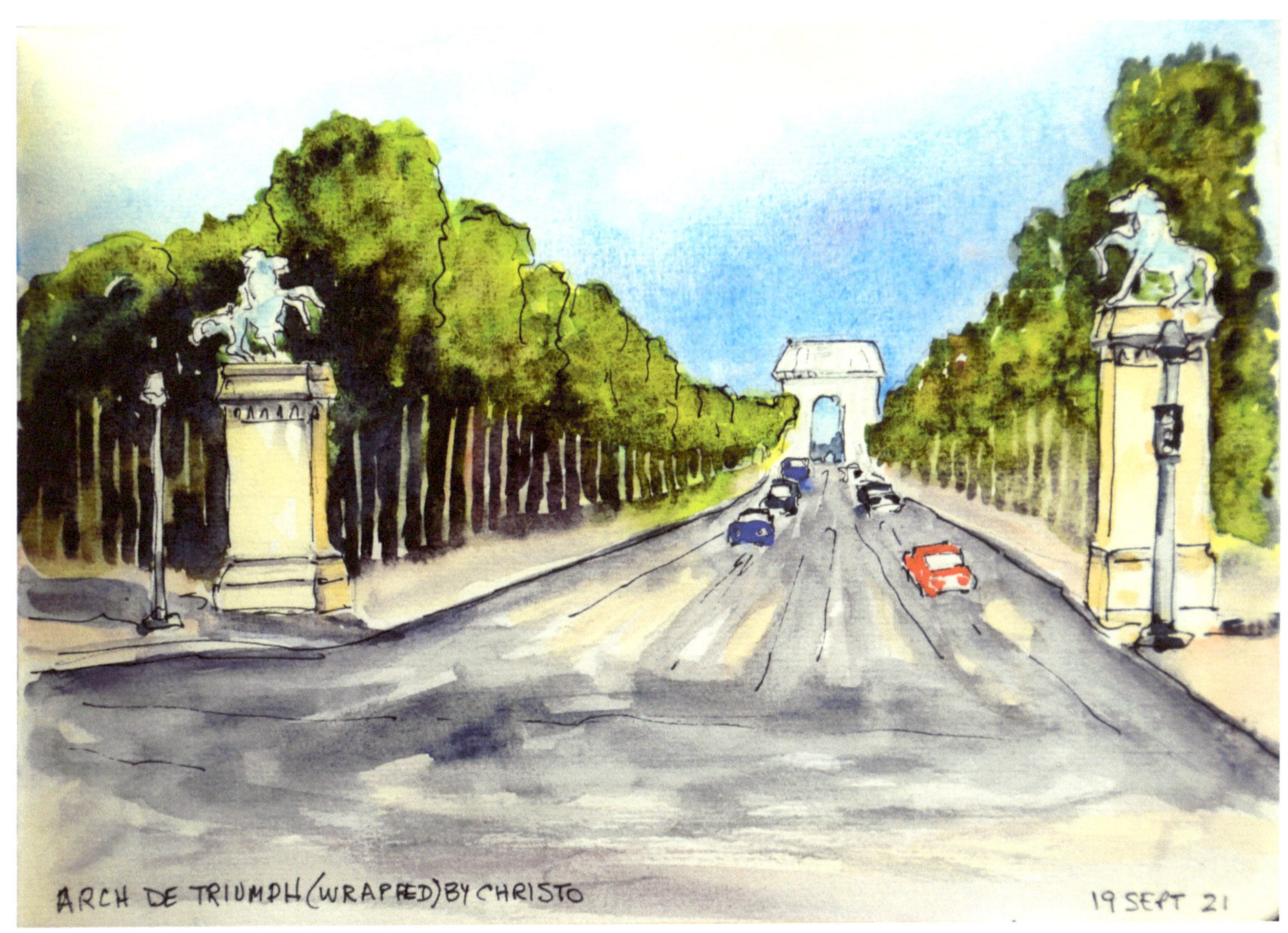

Arc de Triomphe, Paris
I hit the streets at daybreak and arrived at the fountain at the end of the Champs-Elysees with early morning light and almost no traffic. From a distance, there seemed to be no discernable detail on the Arc. I found out later that it had been "draped" by Christo's wife and assistants since he had recently died.

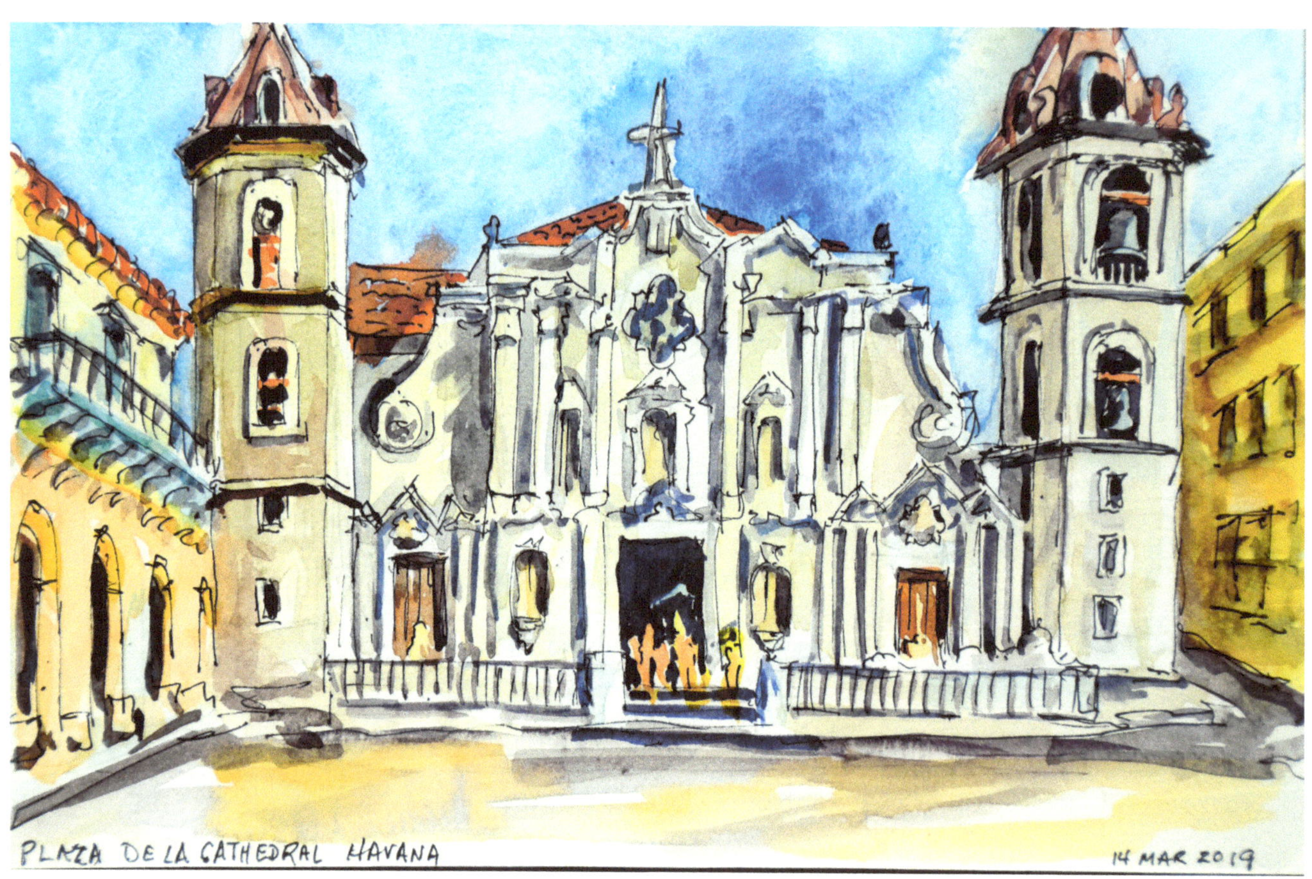

Havana, Cuba

We were fortunate enough to get to Havana just before the cutoff of US travel to the country. It was a paradox....two economies, one for the tourists and Communist Party members and one for the rest of the country. Beautifully restored buildings in the tourist areas and crumbling, falling into ruins buildings in Old Havana where the locals lived. Despite all this, most of the locals welcomed the tourists, always trying to sell something. In the Plaza de la Cathedral, I had a most interesting experience. While painting a sketch of the cathedral, a young Cuban man came up and started a conversation, speaking fluent English. He was studying in a Cuban college to become an architect and loved the old structures, and was intrigued by what I was doing. We had a long talk, mostly non-political, and shared our passion for architecture. More often than not, someone will stop and watch what I'm doing and usually they are locals.

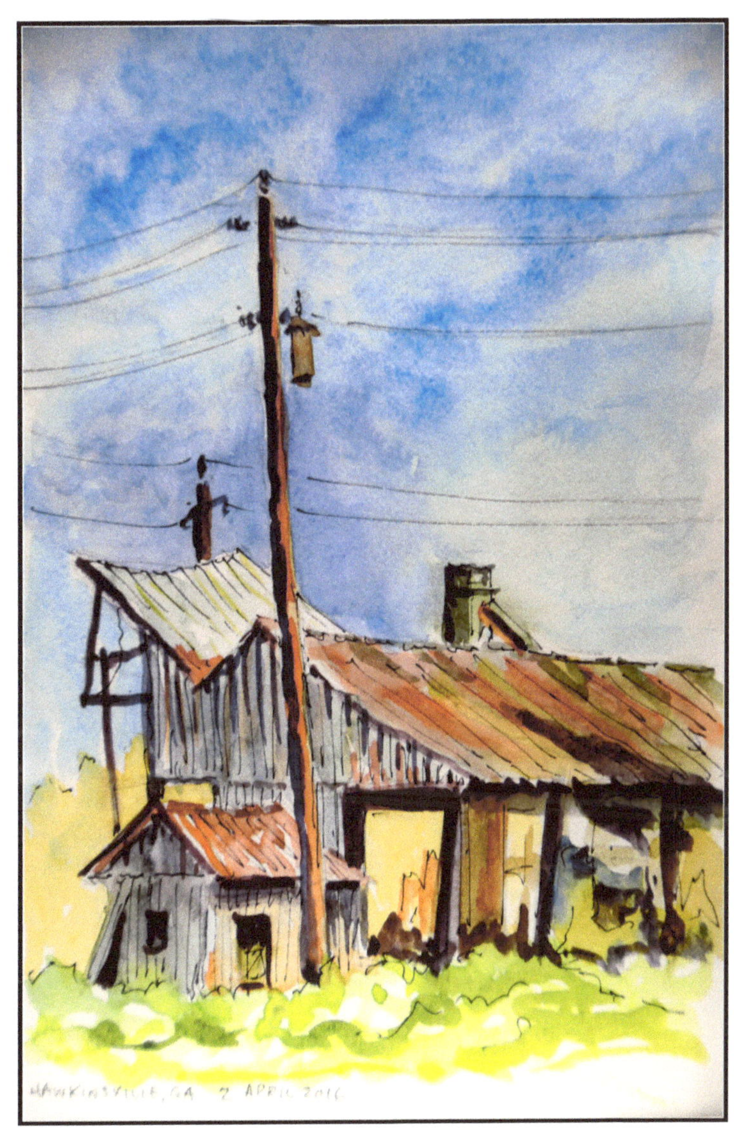

Hawkinsville Ga

You can find subject matter anywhere.....this is an abandoned peanut processing facility in Hawkinsville, GA. My wife and her relatives went to visit their family cemetary while I scouted around and found this old building to paint. I found it interesting because of the lighting (bright highlights and cast shadows) and interesting shapes. All of my subjects take less than an hour to complete, many in 30 minutes or less. It starts with a one minute sketch, then quick watercolor, and final details with pen and ink!

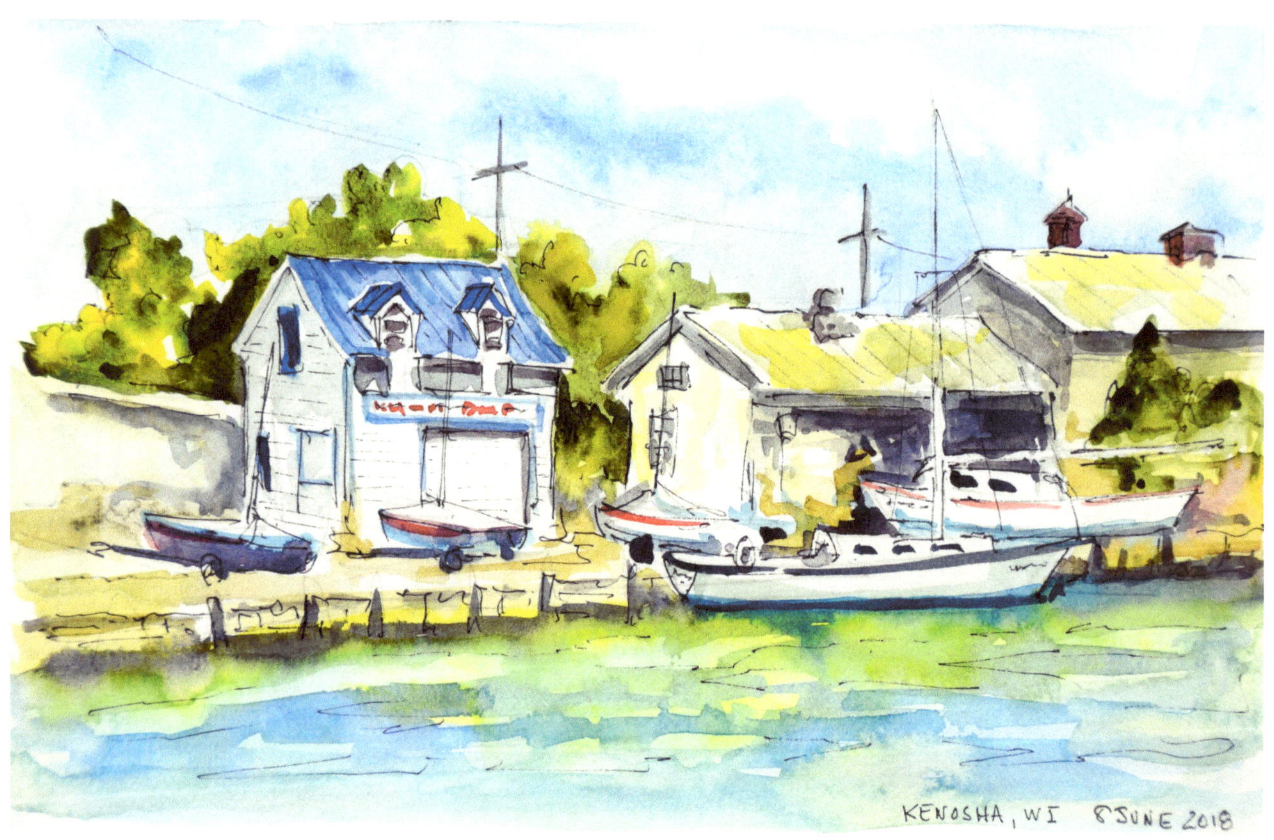

Kenosha, WI

Kenosha, WI is an attractive small town on the shores of Lake Michigan and has been the exhibition venue for Transparent Watercolor Society of America for many years. When I flew to Kenosha to attend the opening reception to receive my Signature Member Award, I took my journal with me. The host hotel and exhibit area were in view of a small harbor coming in from the lake.   I had extra time and managed to do several sketches while there. This is one of them. Boatyards are always a good source for sketches, but sometimes you have to simplify and leave out some of the boats or move them around to improve the composition!

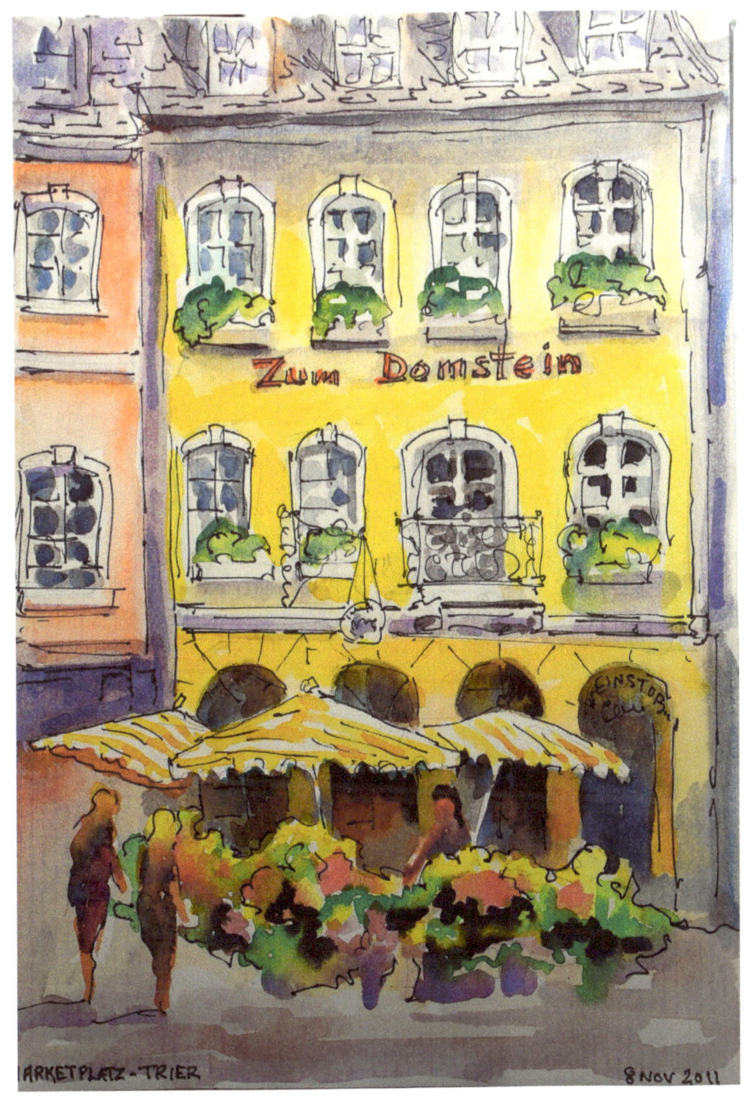

Trier, Germany

Our river boat anchored a short distance from the Bavarian town of Trier, Germany. The walk along the river was scenic, but the marketplace in Trier attracted me far more. The old architecture and the outdoor vendors worked well together. This is a scene of a large flower stand that was drawing many customers. I just sat back on a park bench and enjoyed the local interactions while I painted. You will find that you will remember virtually everything that went on around you while you paint....very unlike trying to remember where you took a photograph!

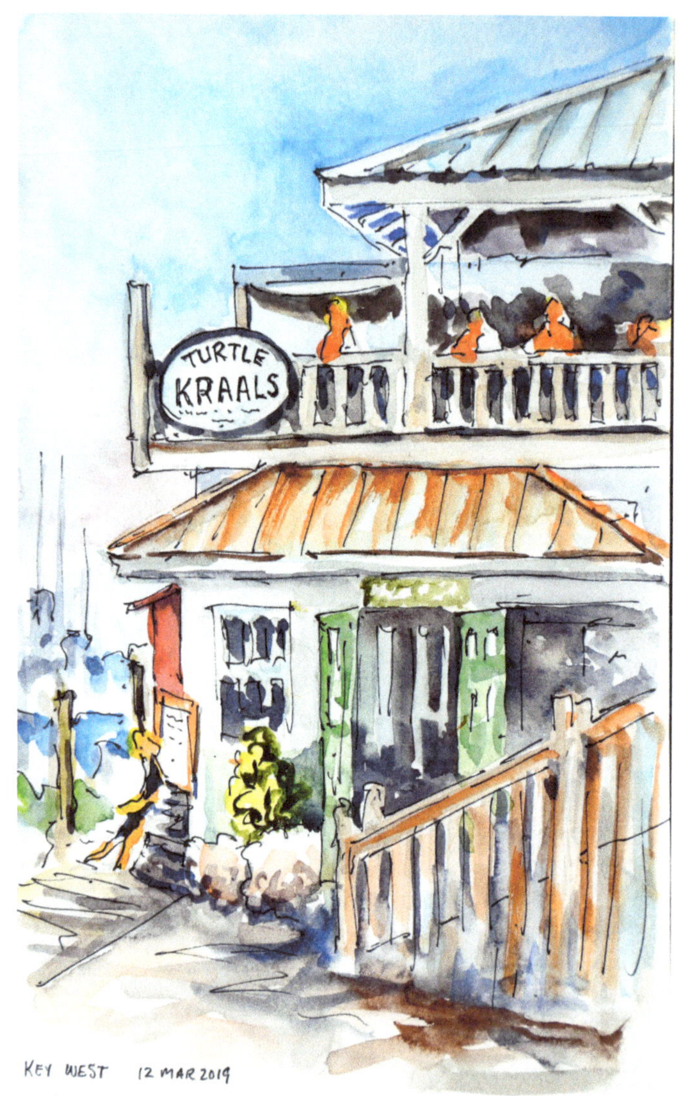

Key West-Turtles Kraals

On a cruise to Havana, Cuba, we stopped in Key West which is also very scenic, but is suffering from too many visitors. In this instance, I walked around most of the town, did several sketches, and have included this one of "Turtle Kraals". This is a popular local bar and grill on the marina side of town. I remember this sketch in particular because I had a young girl stand by me and watch until I was finished while her parents stood patiently nearby. In this sketch, I utilize only general impressions of people as you don't have time to do any real detail. Don't get hung up and waste your time trying to do portrait detail on your figures!

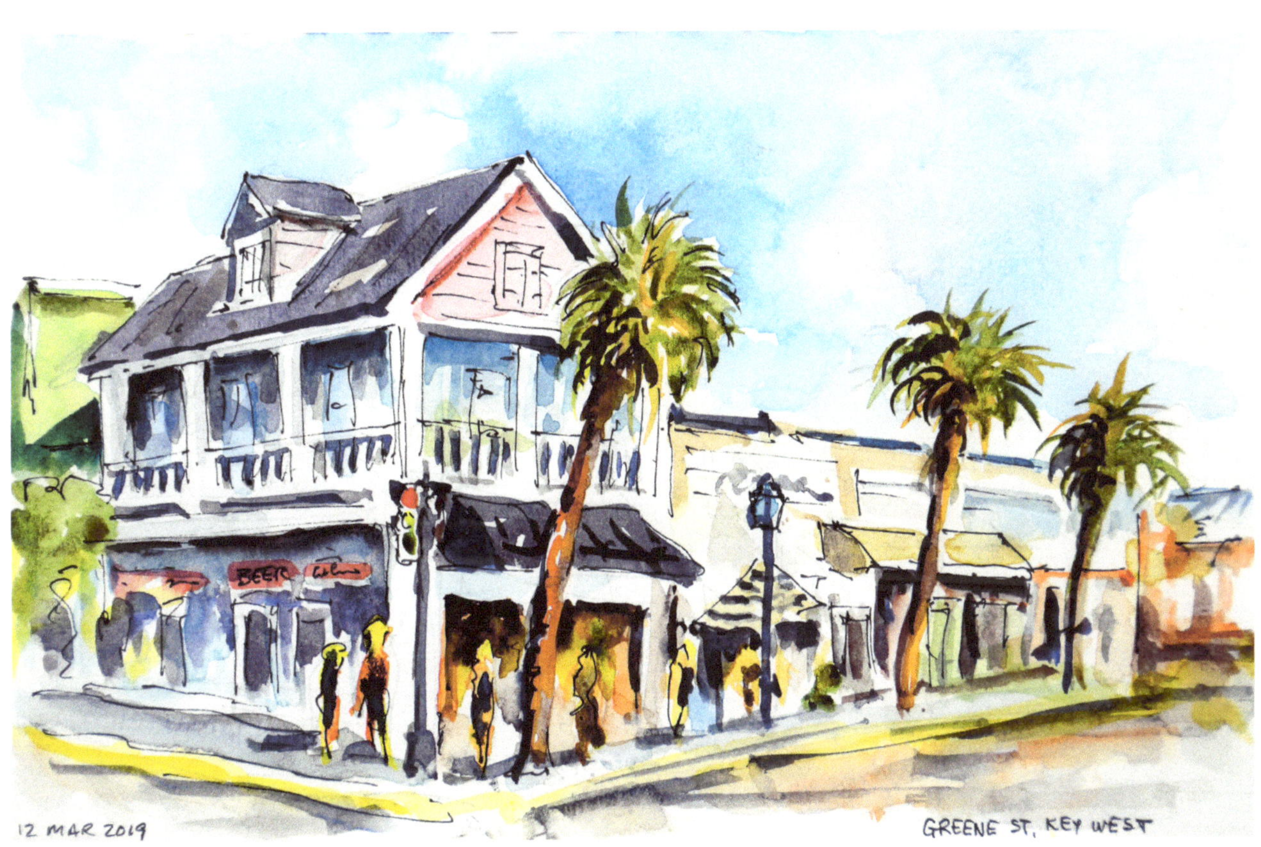

Key West, FL

Key West, as I mentioned before, is quite picturesque and many times overrun by tourists. This view is on Greene Street just before many of the shops opened early one morning. Two ladies in my local watercolor class were traveling with my wife and I, and they tried their hand at plein air journaling alongside me. Street scenes such as this just have to have people in them! Try to make them dynamic and not static, with as little detail as possible.

Lisbon, Portugal
Lisbon, Portugal was one of the most interesting cities I have ever visited, architecturally and it's people. We spent 3 extra days in Lisbon, staying in a small European hotel, just one block from the main square. Every day, I would go to the square and take pictures of different and unusual people as well as doing sketches. I have done at least 10 studio paintings of these people which have been in shows around the country, many having won awards. This view is facing the archway which goes down the most famous pedestrian street in Lisbon, straight to the plaza that I frequented. The bay and harbor is to my back.

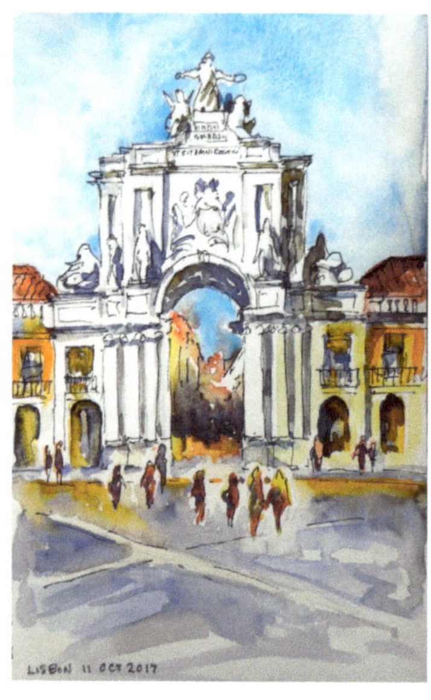

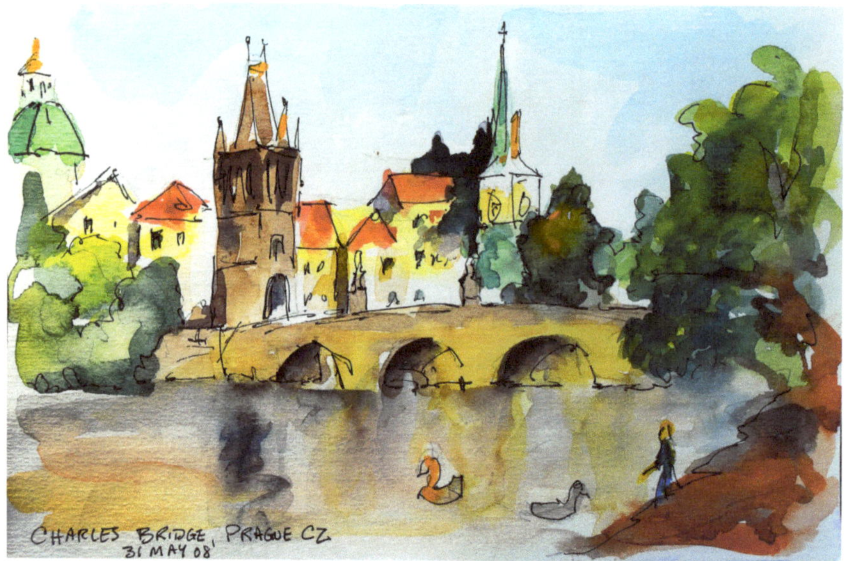

Prague

This sketch from Prague is one of my most memorable ones for several reasons, but mainly because of the interaction with the local population. We had been on a group tour into the Old Town of Prague and split up after the tour was over. I crossed over the Charles Bridge into the part of town where mostly locals lived and tourists didn't venture. Looking for a scene to paint, I found a small park on the water, looking back toward the Old Town and Charles Bridge. The park was full of locals, but I did find an empty seat on a park bench (in the shade!) with a perfect view next to an elderly lady. I sat down next to her , and as I worked, she kept sneaking a peek at what I was doing. When I finished, I turned the journal toward her and showed her the result....I will never forget what happened. She jumped up, hugged me, and called all of the other people in the park to come over. They shook my hand, patted me on the back and congratulated me....all occurring with none of us understanding the other's language!

Cathedral Street, St. Augustine FL
On a visit to my old home town of St. Augustine where I grew up, I did numerous sketches all around the historic area. I chose this view of Cathedral Street near the foot of the Bridge of Lions. St. Augustine was a wonderful place to spend your youth, but the population has skyrocketed from 15,000 to over 300,000 and everyone complains about the traffic and crowding (and expensive prices). On this visit, I managed to get a parking ticket, but I do still have fond memories of all my childhood friends and what St Augustine used to be like!

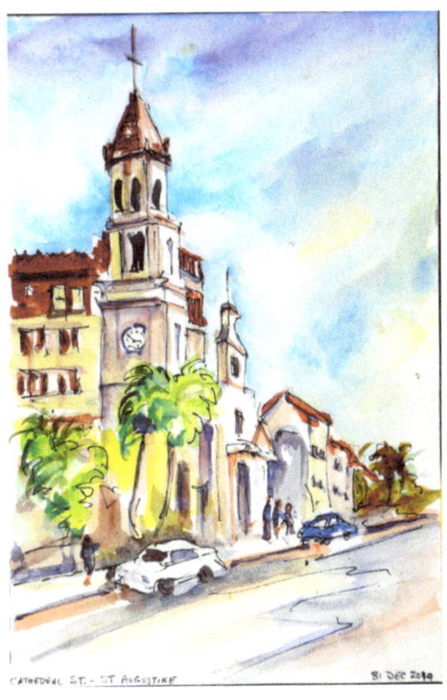

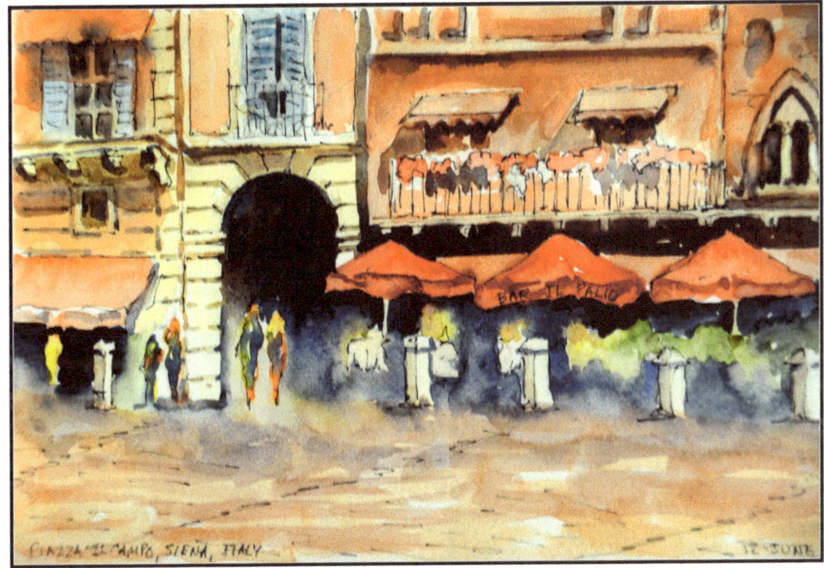

Siena, Italy

Florence seems to be the biggest draw in that area of Italy, but Siena is much more enjoyable because they don't have the huge crush of humanity packing the streets. We spent a week in a villa just outside of Siena which was truly gorgeous.....roses, olive trees, various fruit trees and more! The main plaza in Siena was picturesque and lively, and every year was covered with dirt for a horse race with all of the areas of the city competing. This was their signature event. This image of the Piazzo Il Campo was done sitting at the foot of the church on the opposite side.   This is another example of how to put people in your painting with a minimum of detail.!

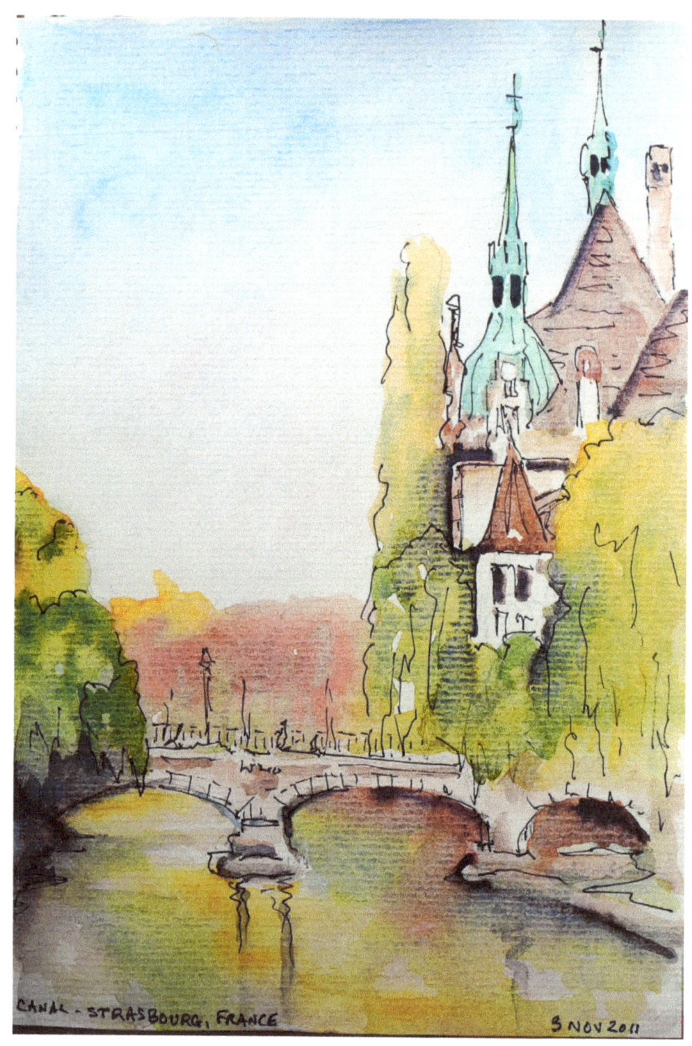

Strasbourg, France

Strasbourg, France is a wonderfully beautiful city of canals. The town has been contested over the centuries by France and Germany, so it has characteristics of both. After taking a tour by small boat around the major canals, we spent some time on our own just walking the streets and this is one of my memorable images. It was early morning and still somewhat misty when I found this scene.   I was impressed by the softness created by the mist, and this is the result.

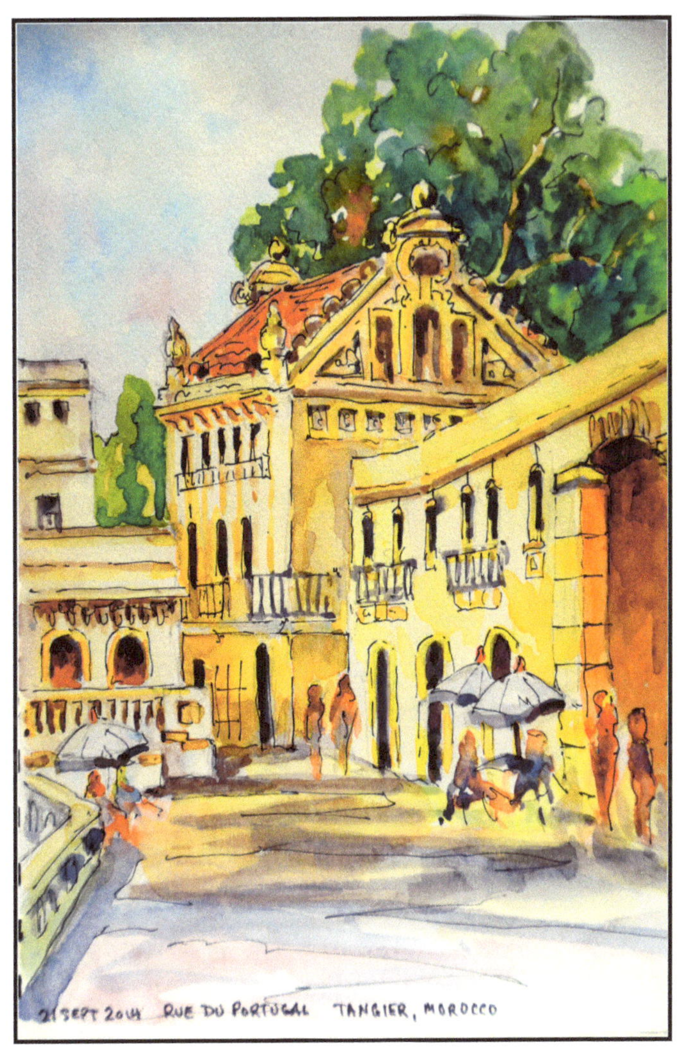

Tangier, Morocco

Tangier, Morocco is interesting in that it has had many influences over the years and therefore it's people are very varied. After getting off the ship at the port, we were deluged with cab drivers, guides, sightseeing offers and more. We really wanted to just walk around, but a young boy about 12 years old kept persisting...he wanted to be our personal guide.   Of course, money was the reason. Finally, after having him tag along for 20 minutes or so, we decided to give him a try. As it turned out, he was quite reliable and knowledgeable. He even patiently waited while I did sketches and took photos. Actually, we really needed him once we got inside the walls of the city, as the streets were winding and confusing, and maps were worthless. A highlight was when he took us to his uncle's spice shop, where we were treated royally and ended up purchasing some spices. This image is the Portuguese embassy in an area close to the harbor.

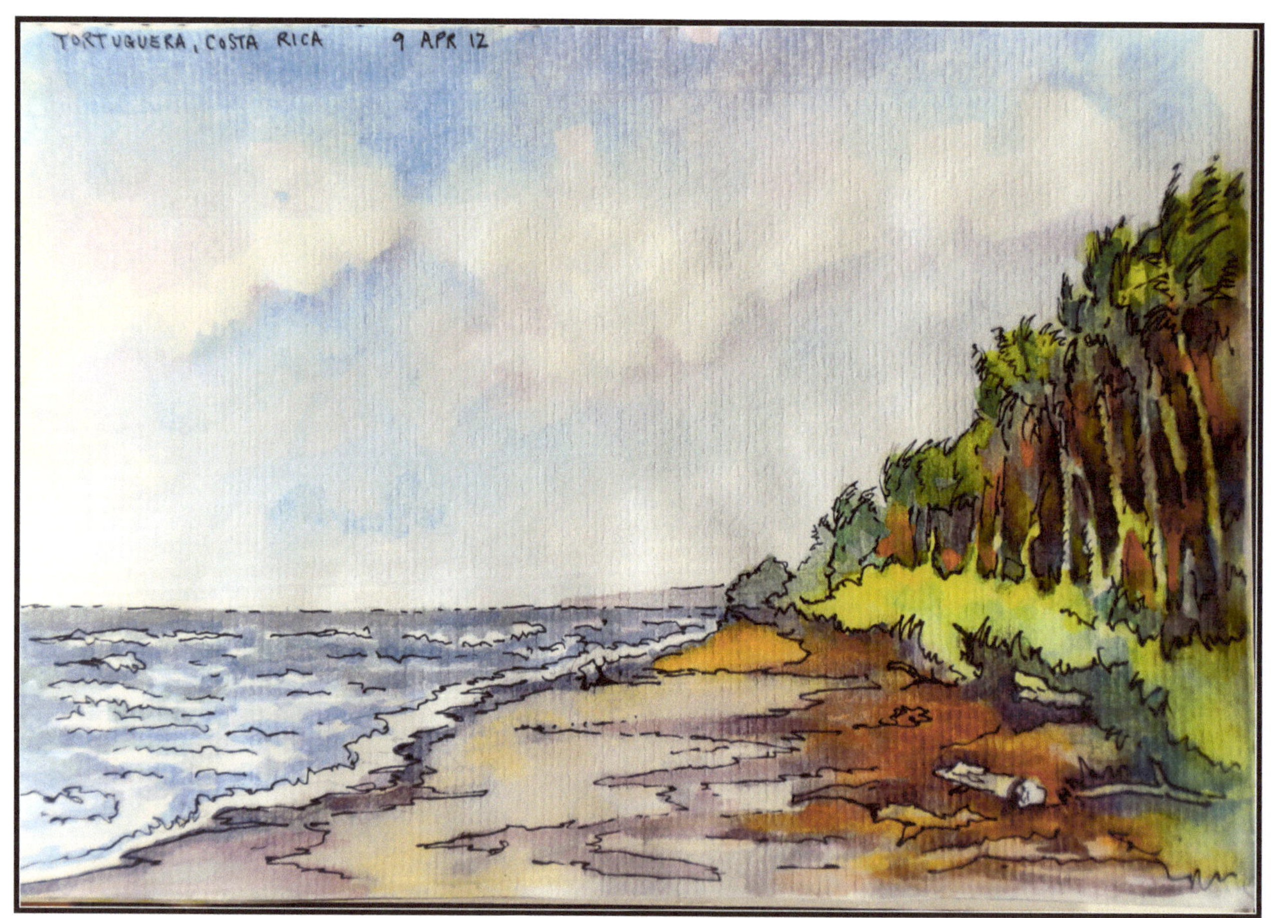

Tortuguero, Costa Rica

Tortuguero, or "Land of the Turtles" is a principal nesting area for the Central American area and has been maintained by the Costa Ricans for many decades. After having seen many beaches in Florida, the Caribbean, and elsewhere, I was surprised at the beaches here. The water is extremely rough and dangerous, and no swimming is allowed. It is also murky and the sand is dark, and the debris washing ashore is unbelievable. The locals blame it on trash dumped overboard by cruise ships, and it is an arduous task trying to pick up the flotsam as it perpetually washes ashore! The turtles seem to still prefer this stretch of the beach to lay their eggs. This sketch will forever remind me of the state of the beach.

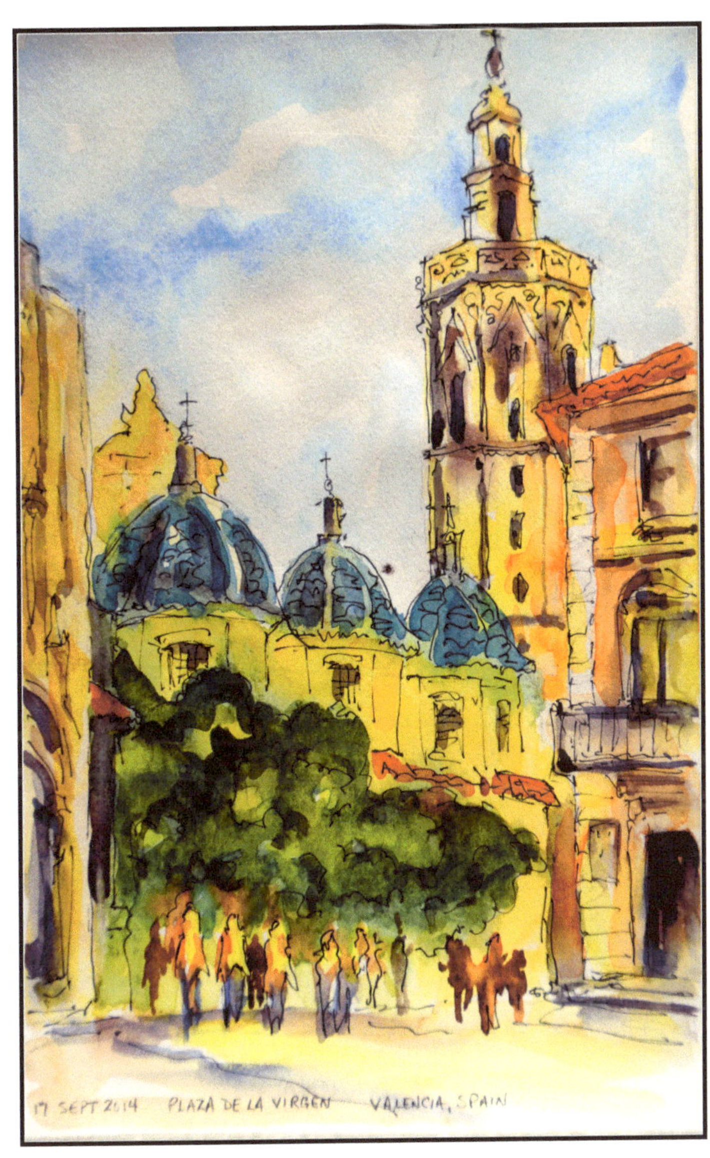

Valencia, Spain
Valencia, Spain had many interesting areas....and as we walked through the historic section of town, I saw several intriguing street scenes with groups of people. This view of the Plaza de la Virgen was the most interesting and had great lighting on a sunny day. Rainy days and sunrise/sunsets, however can produce some very beautiful paintings due to the lighting.

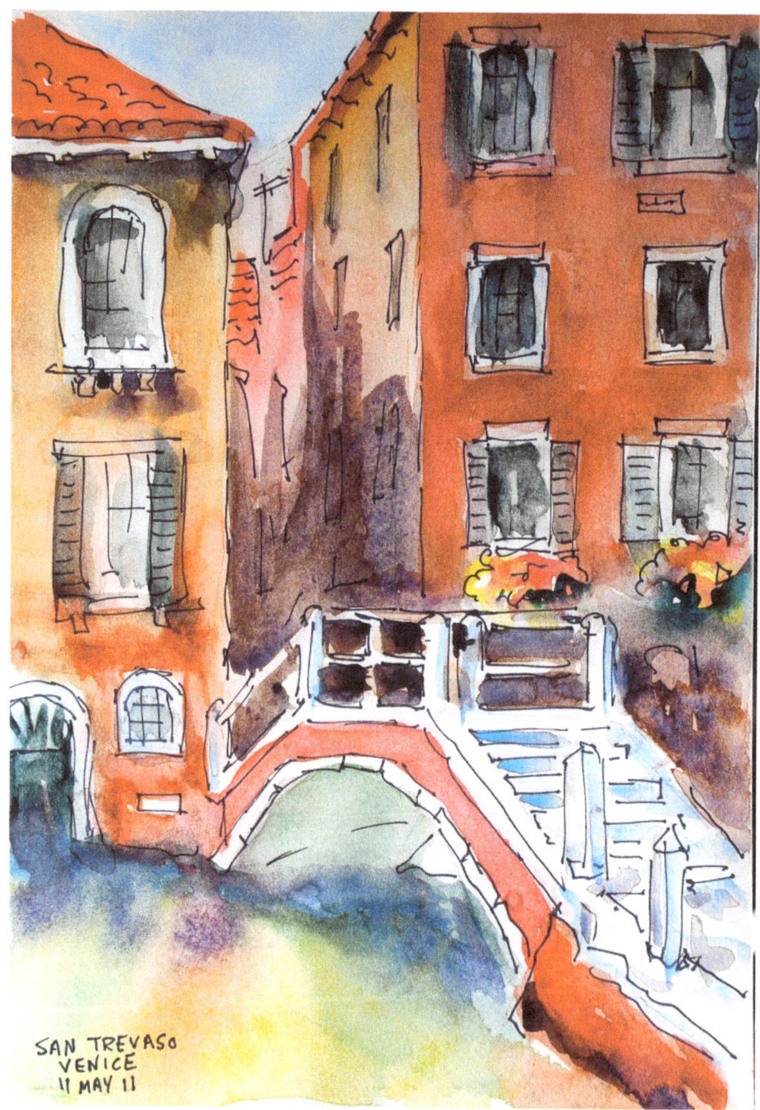

Venice

In Venice, we found so many things that were paintable that it was sometimes hard to decide which...but, in any case, the painting must include a canal. My wife and I stayed in a B&B in San Trevaso, not far from the Doge's Palace. A person can cover all of Venice on foot and it makes it easy to wander around and find a perfect site. This view is from one of the canals close to our B&B.   Venice is another beautiful spot that is being smothered by tourists and cruise ships and is fighting the gradual increase in sea levels. The buildings are still being supported by ancient wooden pilings that are sunk in the mud below.

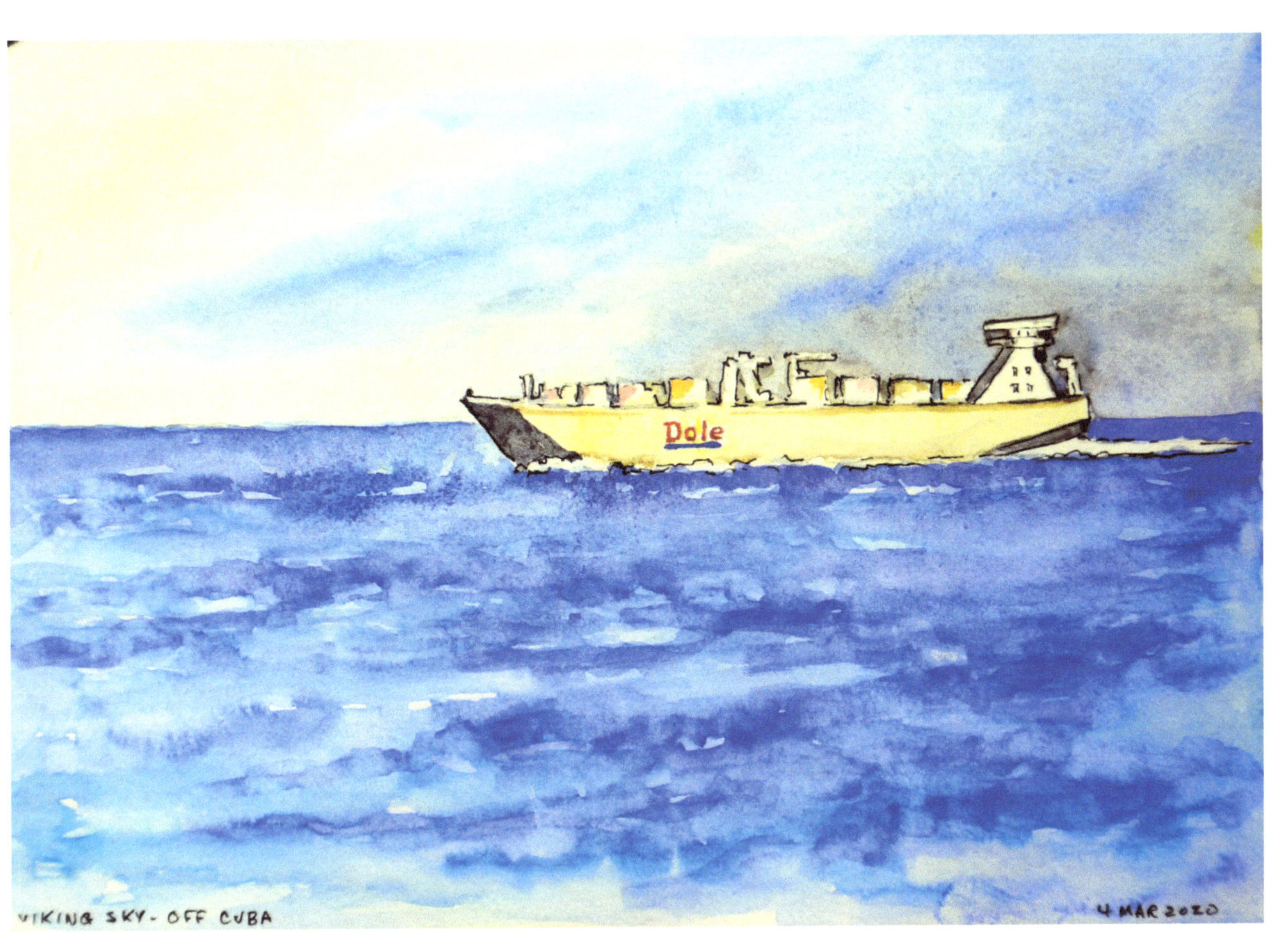

Dole Ship - off Cuba

When your ship is at sea, it's still possible to find something to sketch. My son was traveling with me and we were relaxing having a beer in our room with a veranda. As I glanced outside, I saw our ship was overtaking a Dole container ship just off the coast of Cuba. I grabbed my painting stuff and headed for the veranda. This is another situation where you are trying to hit a moving target. Our ship was rapidly overtaking the other ship, so I just sketched the ship in quickly, got the colors and lighting down, and finished the sky and water after the ship was out of view.

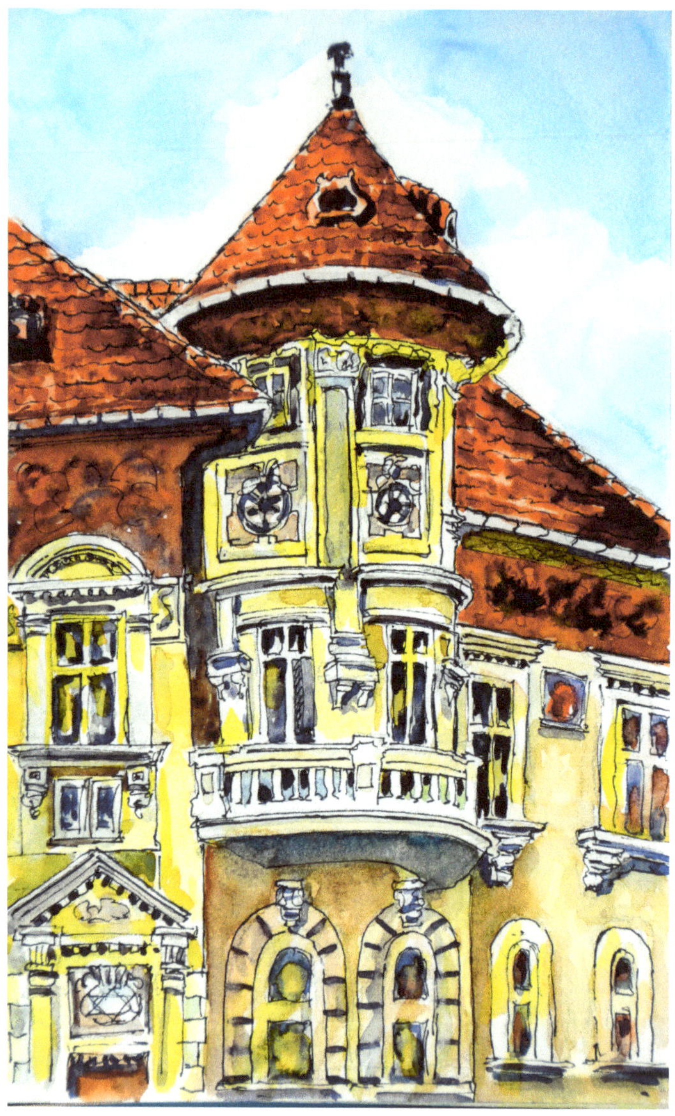

Bucharest
I've included this sketch from Bucharest because it is more involved architecturally than most sketches. This is why I do the pen and ink last, so I can judge how much detail I need to bring out the subject. However, to get the view I wanted with the shadows, I had to sit on the opposite side of the street in the sun. I rapidly became drenched with sweat. It's great when you have a nice spot to paint from in the shade, but that's not always possible, and when you're traveling you can't carry umbrellas, stools, etc. with you most of the time. Therefore, dress in layers and carry sunscreen!

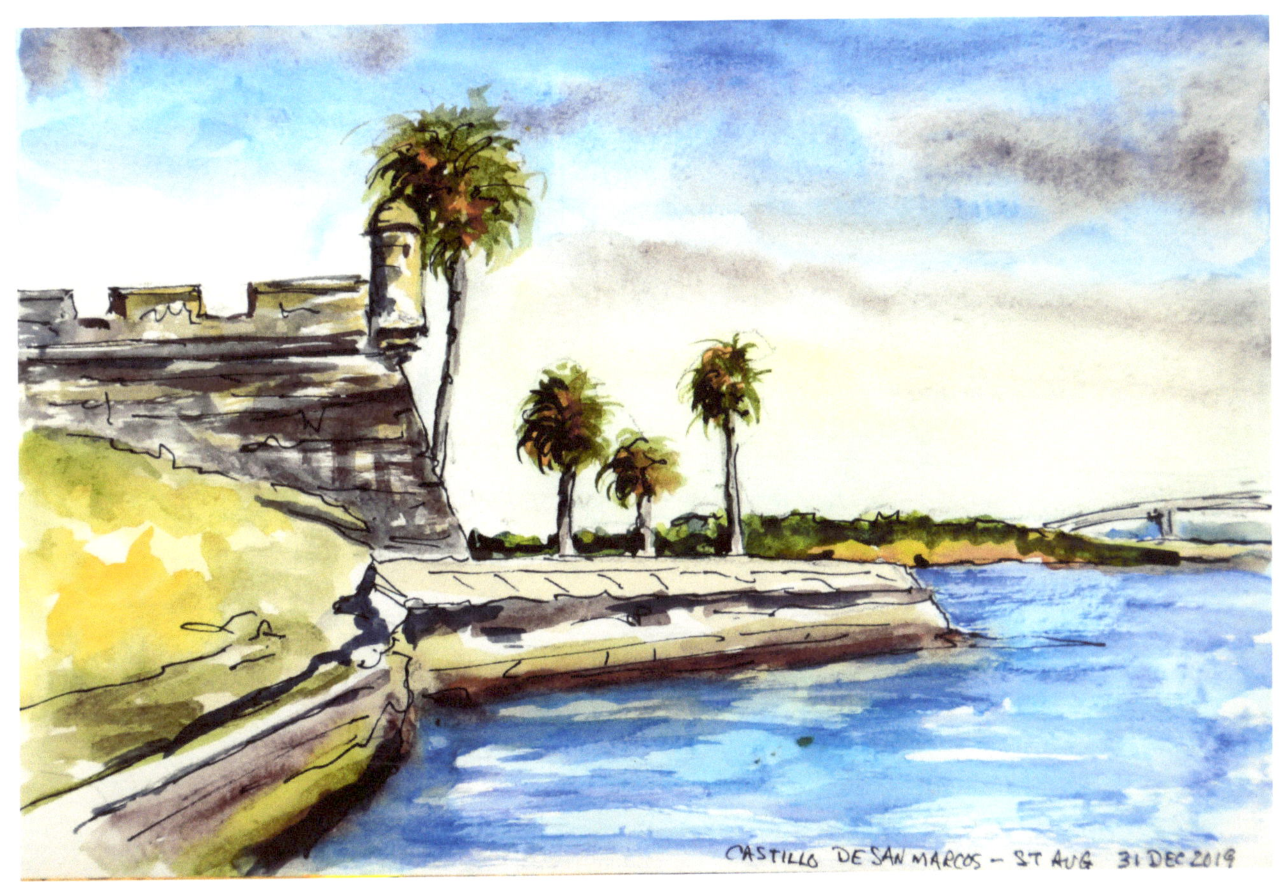

Castillo de San Marcos

In this sketch, I go back to my old home town of St. Augustine, painting what is one of the most painted scenes in town, the Castillo de San Marcos.   When I grew up, everyone just called it the "Old Fort".   In the late 40's and early 50's, I would go to my Boy Scout meetings at the American Legion hall just down Bay Street from the fort. After the meeting, we'd all go down to the fort and rough house on the sloping hills around the fort and sometimes climb the walls where there was no water in the moat. That wouldn't sit very well with the establishment today.

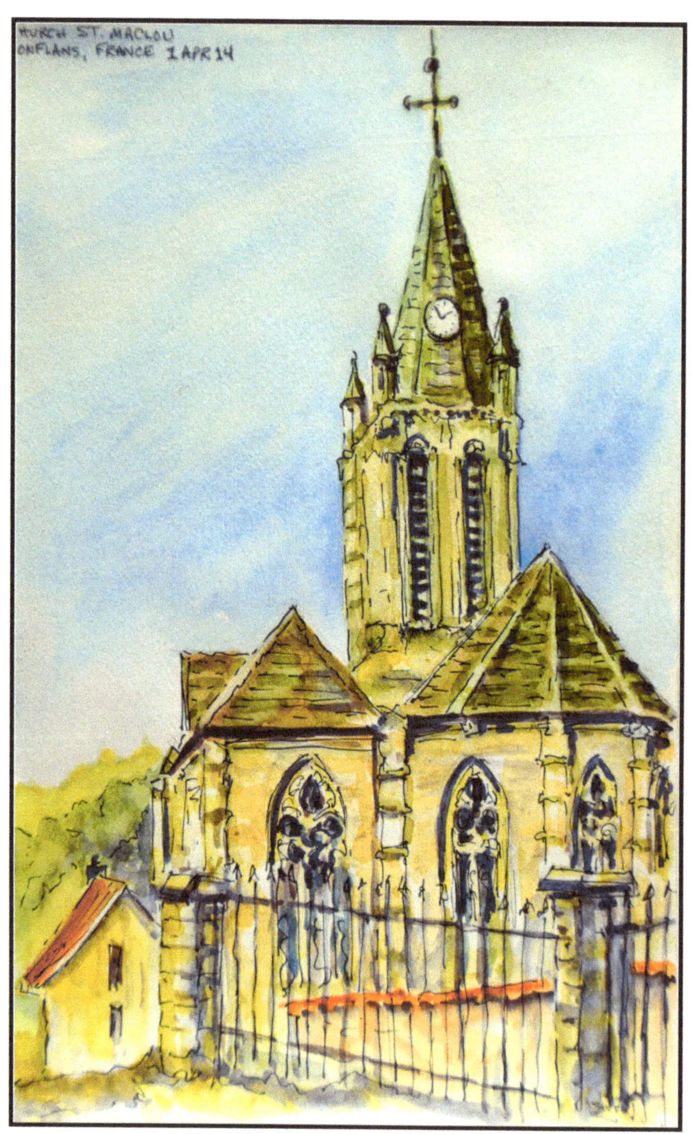

Conflans, France
The river cruise from Paris to Normandy was exceptional, but we did encounter variable weather in March, from cold and rainy to bright and sunny! This painting was done in the nice weather phase. Church St. Maclou in Conflans, France was on the way to Normandy. We also had good weather at the memorial sites in Normandy and it was truly an emotional and humbling experience! If you ever have the chance, please go!

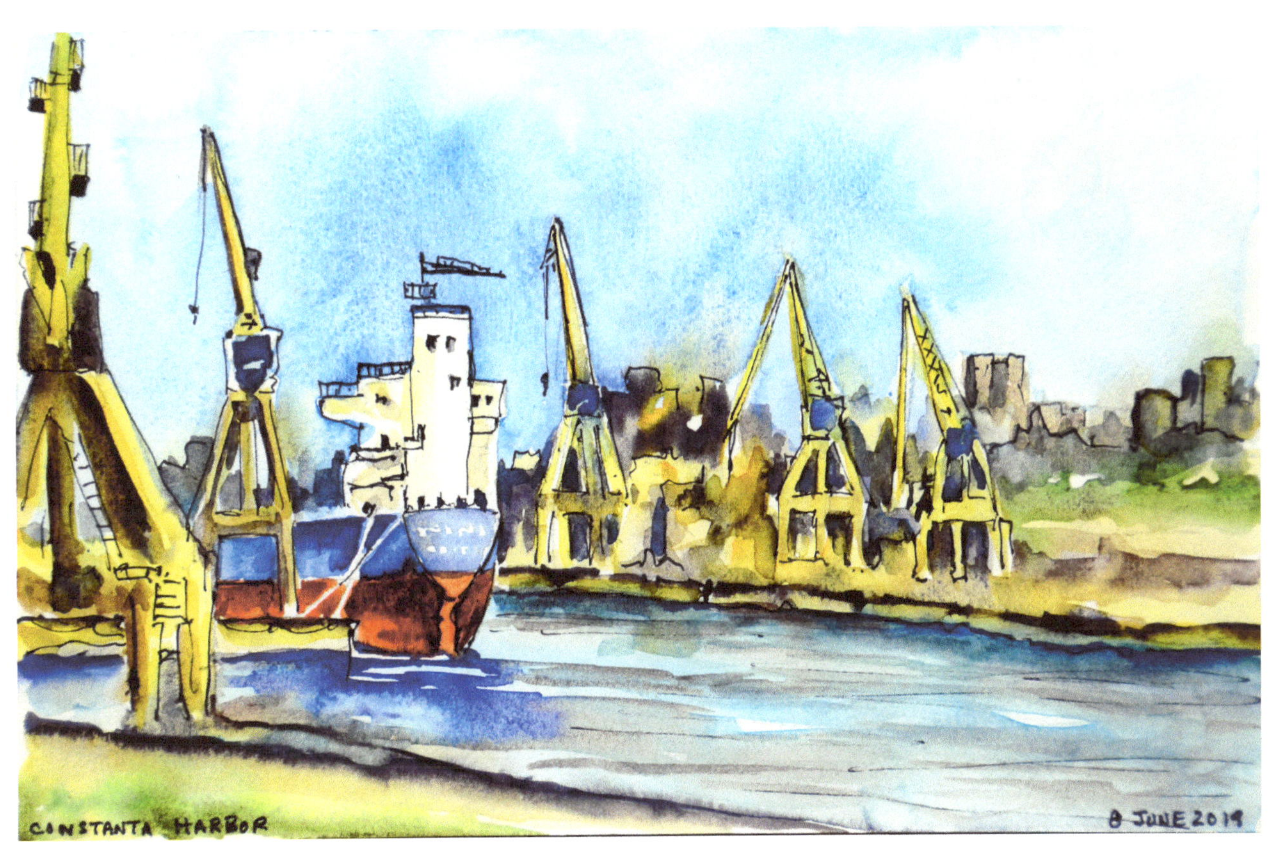

Constanta Harbor

This sketch of Constanta Harbor is a good example of how you can do a painting without leaving the ship.   Our river boat from the Danube left the river and took us on a short trip into the harbor. From a viewpoint on the upper decks, I was able to find an interesting view of the harbor. The bright blue and red colors of the ship helped create an excellent center of interest. Always remember that there are scenes everywhere around us if you just look!

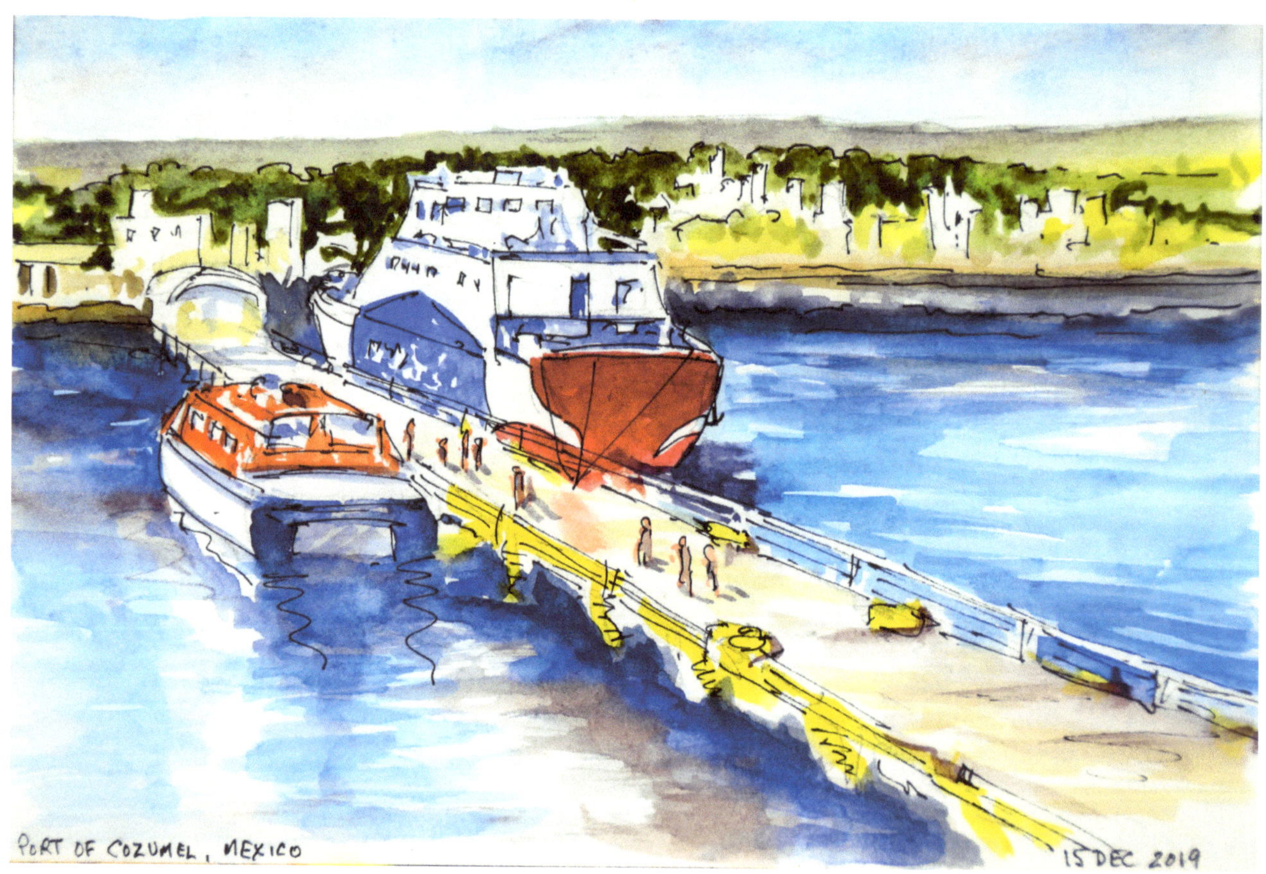

Cozumel, Mexico

This view of the port at Cozumel, Mexico is another good example of what you might find without leaving the ship. Actually, I had come back a bit early from an excursion and had some time before our ship left, so I went to the upper decks to get a better view and found this. The two anchored ships provide the center of interest with their placement and bright colors and the diagonal pier leading to them. Often you will not have time when you're with a group to do any sketches, so look for opportunities like this when you get back!

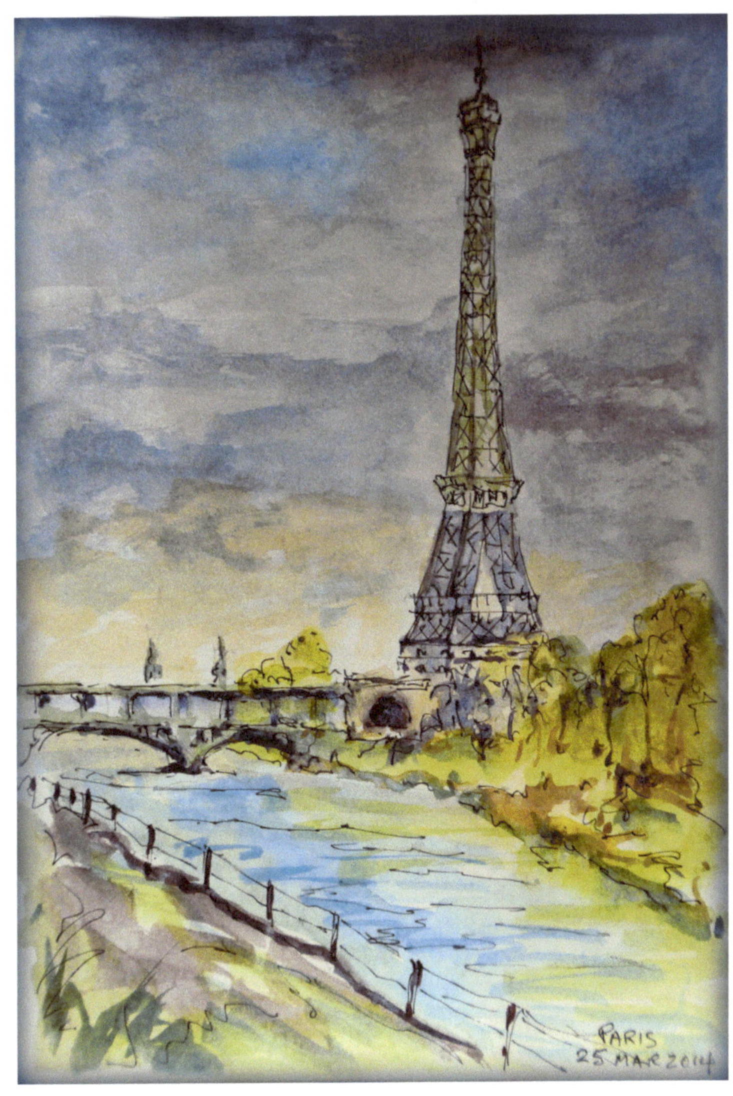

Eiffel in the Rain

"Eiffel in the Rain" was done in Paris before we boarded the boat to Normandy.   We stayed in a very tiny hotel room just opposite the Eiffel tower, across the Seine. It was very cold with a light rain, but Louisa tagged along as we walked along the banks of the Seine. I found one of the bridges down river that had a road along the river bank. We were able to get under the bridge (and out of the rain) and use that as a vantage point from which to paint. As I mentioned, painting in the rain is not particularly enjoyable, but sometimes the results can be effective. You have to remember that watercolors take much longer to dry when it's cold and wet, so plan ahead!

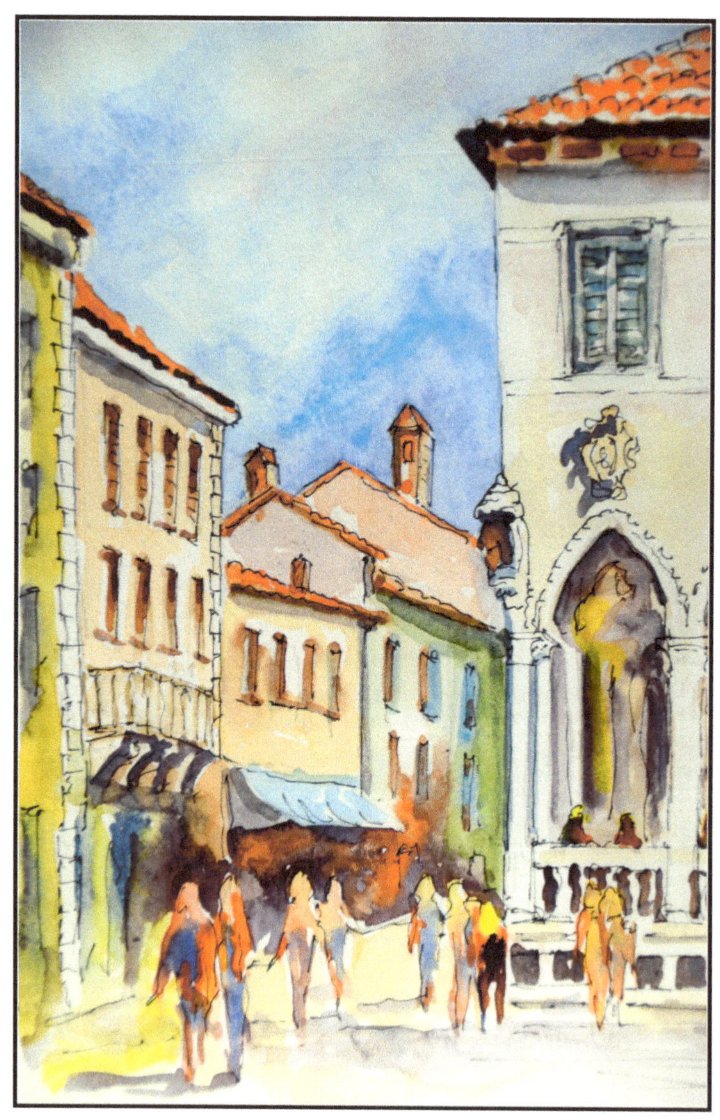

Koper, Slovenia

Koper, Slovenia is a picturesque town that's not on most people's radar, but I found it to be very intriguing. After wandering around looking for just the right spot, I found this street scene that appealed to me. Many times you will not be able to find an ideal position to work from or a comfortable place to sit, especially on a busy street. I have worked standing up, using a window ledge to support my journal, with barely enough room to support my palette. The key word is "improvise"!

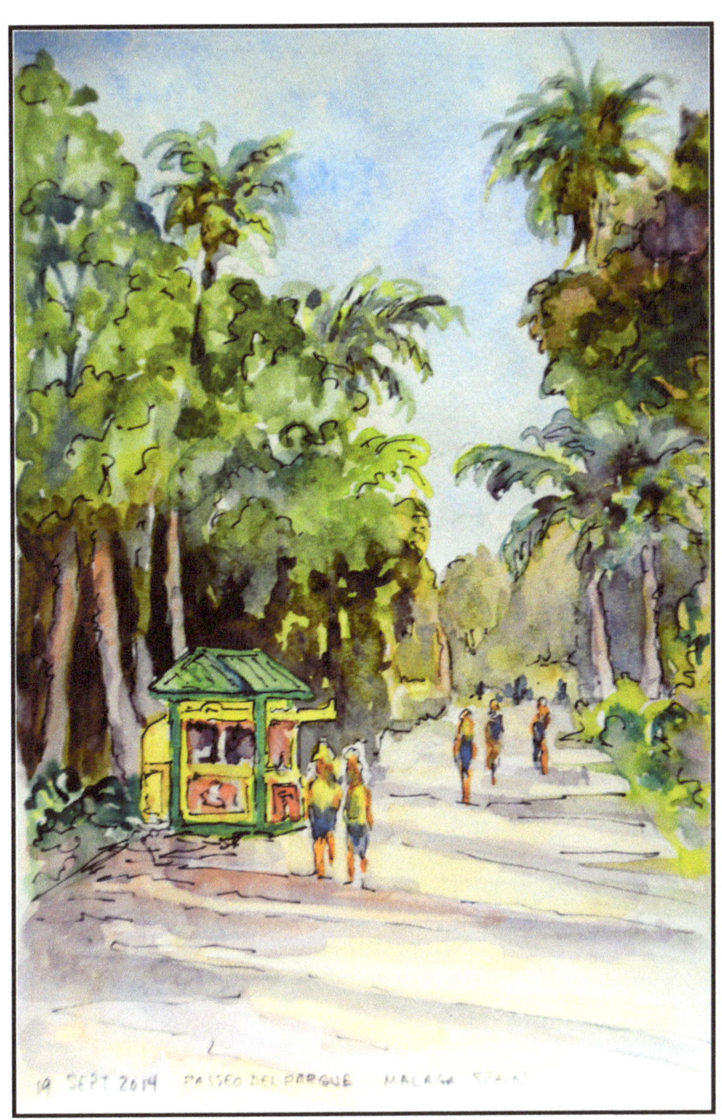

Malaga, Spain

Many times you will walk by a particular scene and not recognize the potential. This happened to me in Malaga, Spain. I had left the ship and gone into the town. Several things sort of appealed to me, but nothing really stood out.   On the way back to the ship as I was walking through the park adjacent to the harbor, I glanced around and spotted this view. I thought it demonstrated how the locals spent their time away from the tourist crowds. It's another good example of how putting people in a street scene helps bring it to life!

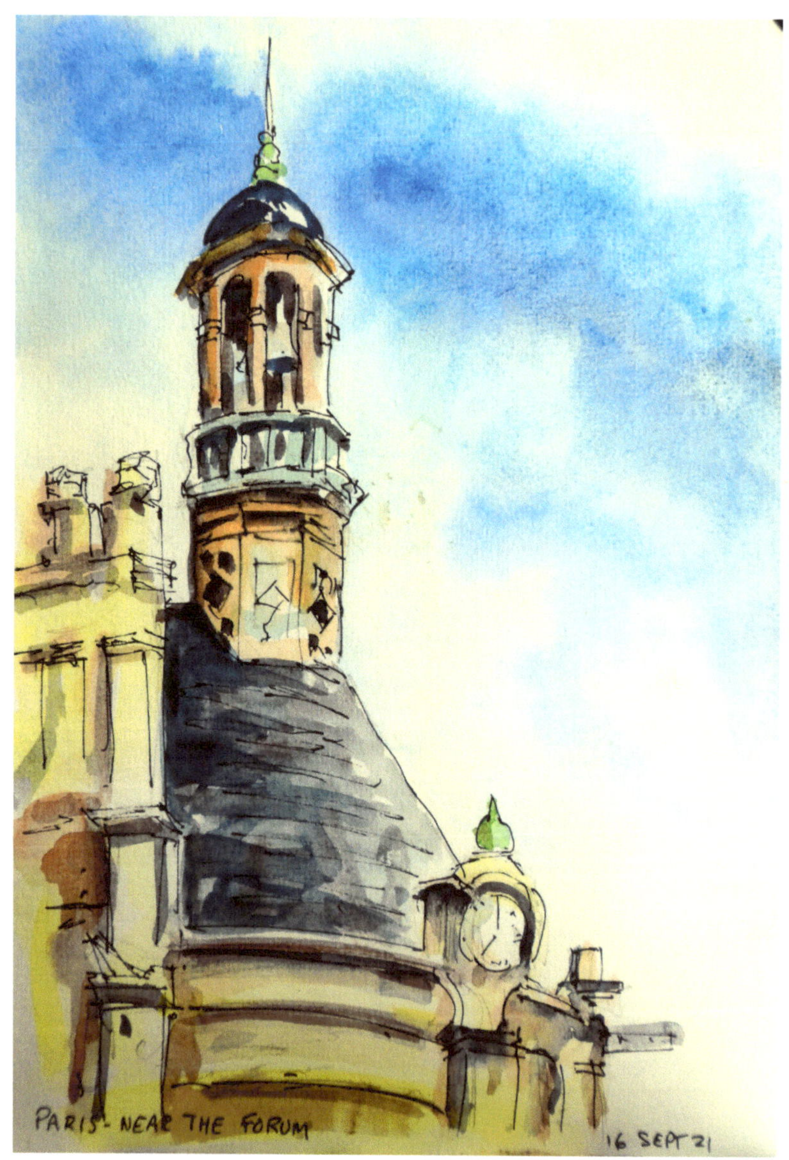

Paris-Near the Forum
There is one more image from Paris that I'd like to include.....one that is relatively simple and can be done quickly.   Spires, arches and domes are always interesting and they can be done without including the whole building.   This image is from a building near the forum in Paris that I found worthy of painting!

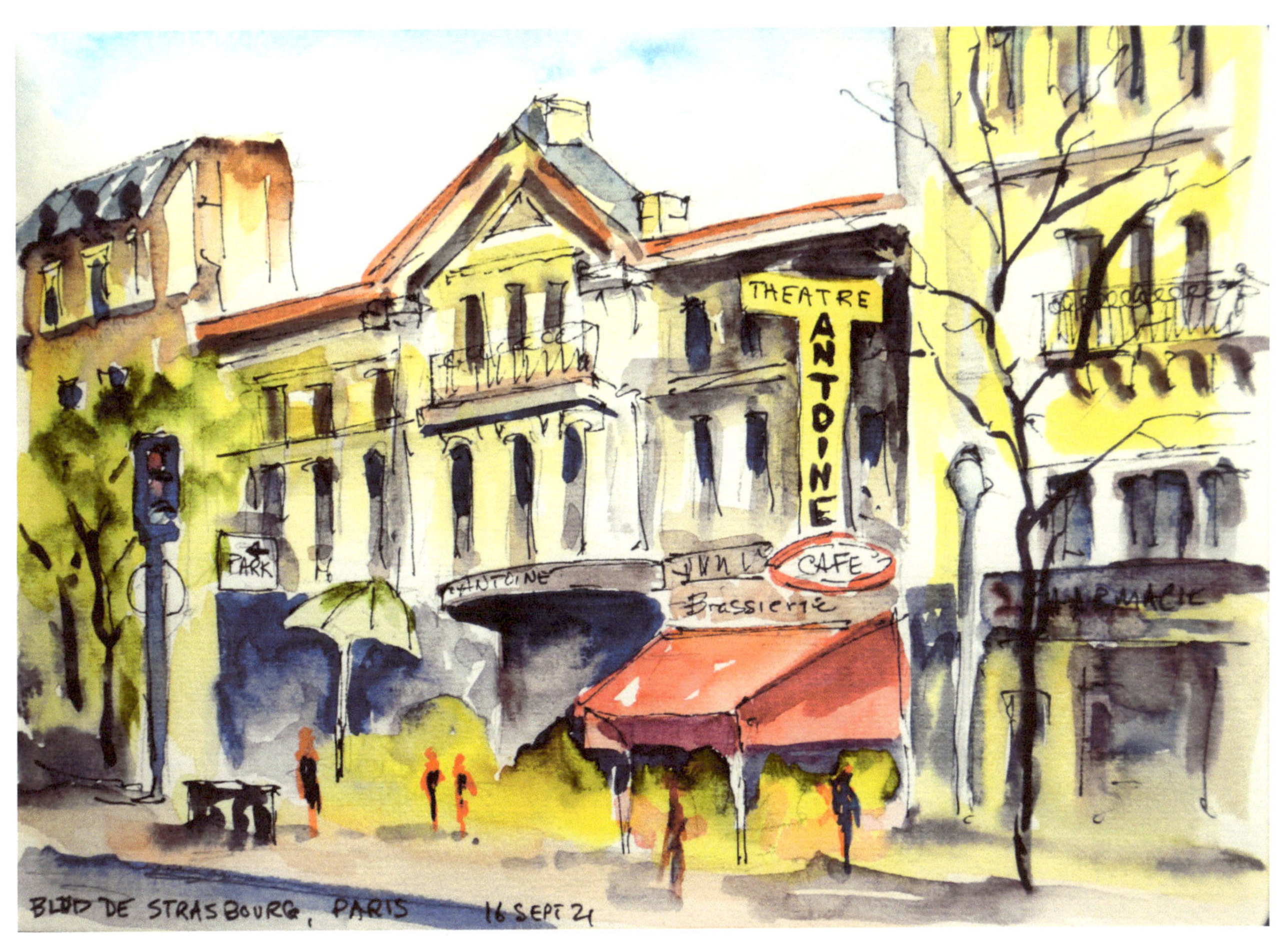

Blvd de Strasbourg, Paris

*There were so many places to paint in Paris, it's hard to pick a favorite! I included this sketch because I went by it so many times....
Blvd de Strasbourg was a main thoroughfare about one block away from my apartment that I took many times heading to another part
of town. It was always active and busy, day or night.   I took many photo shots as well of interesting people along the sidewalks.   Just
across the street was the health clinic where I got my Covid-19 test to get back in the US!*

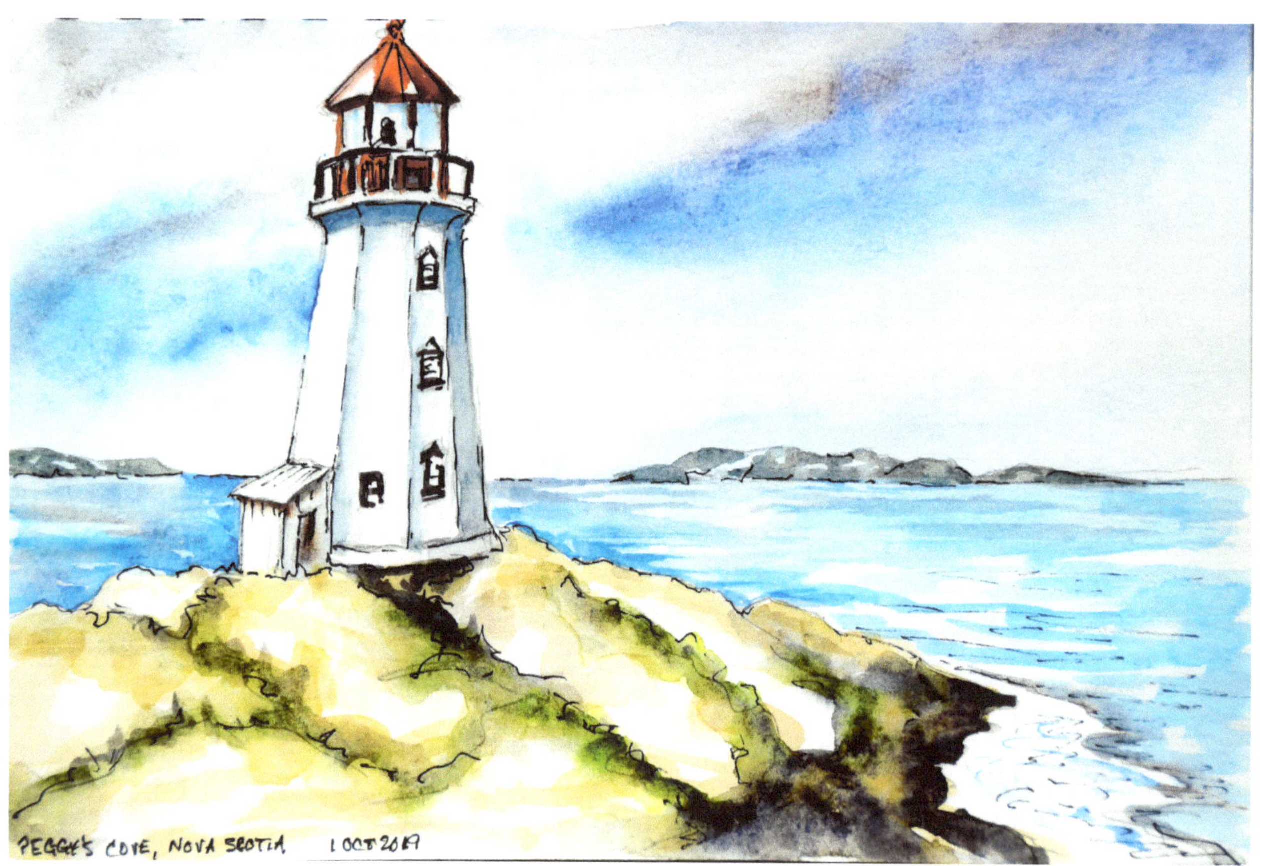

Peggy's Cove Lighthouse

At some point I suppose we perhaps need to include famous sites...in this case, we probably have the most photographed and/or painted scene in the world. That is, of course, Peggy's Cove lighthouse. It was quite scenic and over run by tourists, so I had to ignore all the masses of people on all sides of the lighthouse! This is a problem in many places when you can't find a view without being obstructed. I do much prefer finding a place without quite so many people!

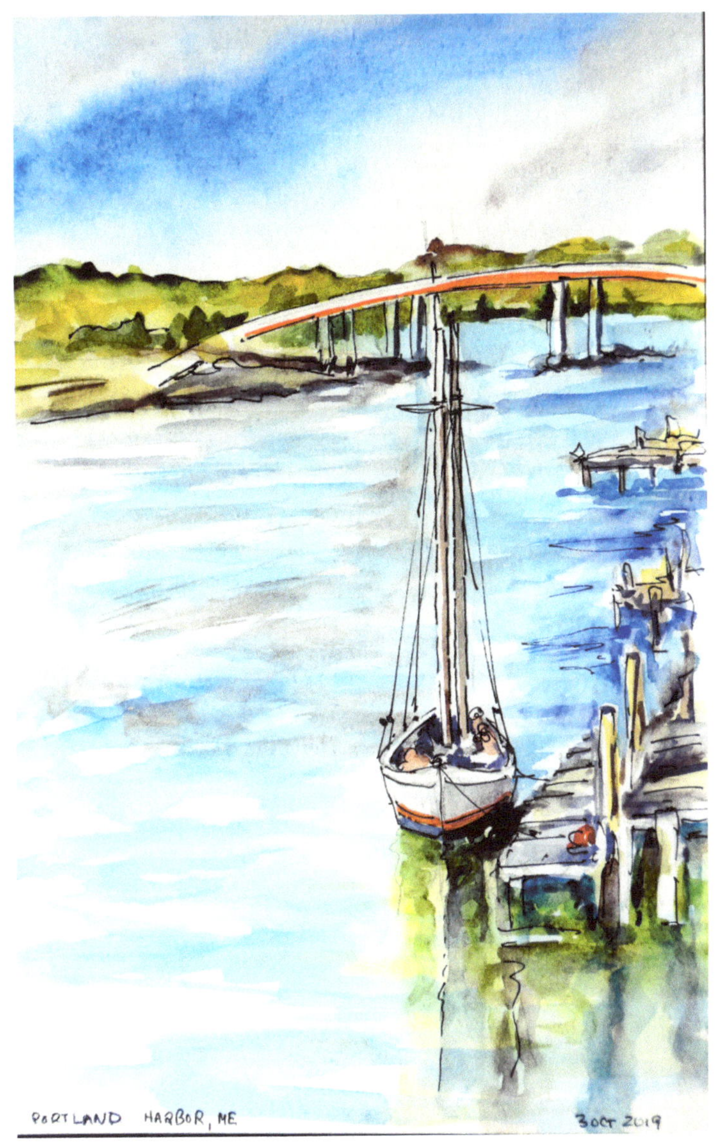

Portland, ME

The Portland, ME harbor had a plethora of scenes to paint. Some were onshore, and others could be seen right from the boat. This is one that was readily available from my cabin veranda. Remember, always look for a center of interest, just like you would do in a studio painting. As I get older, I tend to look for more of these scenes that I can paint from a comfortable position. However, some of my favorites were found after miles of walking!

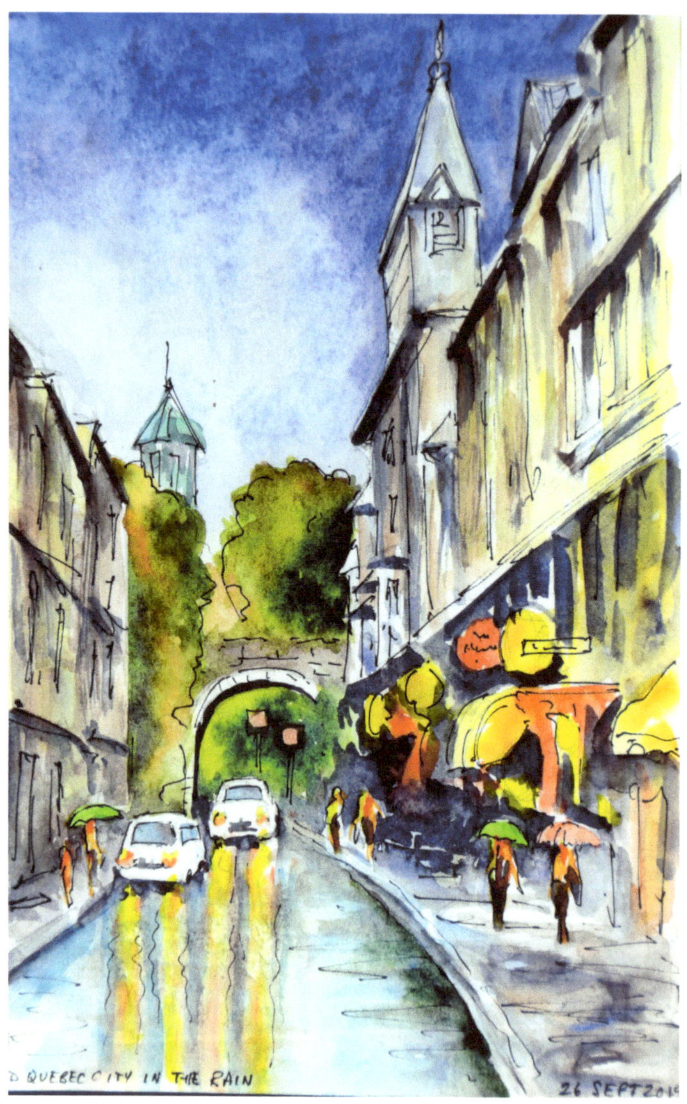

Quebec City

Painting in the rain isn't very much fun, but sometimes you have a scene that you just can't pass up. This sketch of "Quebec City in the Rain" is one of them.   My wife and I were with another couple walking from awning to overhang to keep from getting too wet. I had to try to do this scene because the water reflections on the street and umbrellas and awnings are what really made it.   I quickly did the sketch and watercolors, then we popped into a bistro for lunch and I finished the pen & ink there.

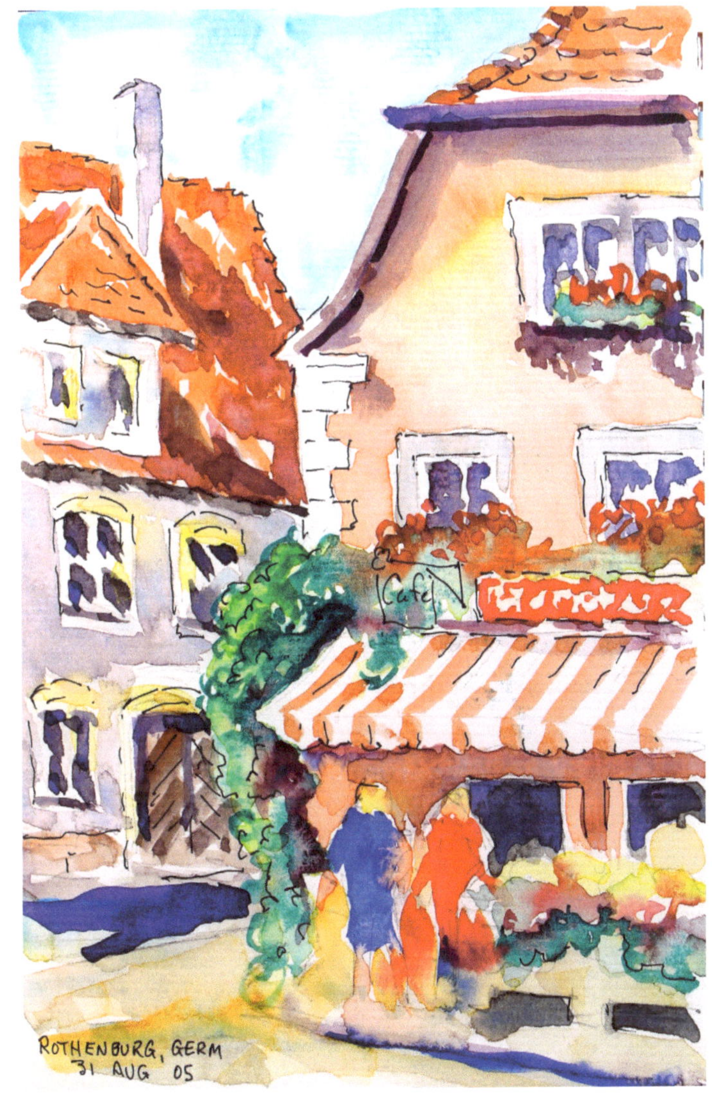

Rothenburg, Germany

When you are traveling, you never know what may happen....in some cases, it turns out better than you would ever imagine! This sketch from Rothenburg, Germany is a result of an encounter on the narrow gauge railroad from Cusco, Peru to Machu Picchu. My wife and I met a young German couple on the train, and as we approached the end at Machu Picchu, the young couple realized they didn't have the necessary cash to get into the park. I loaned him the cash, we stayed in touch and a couple of years later we did a home exchange with us staying in his apartment in Augsburg. We drove over much of Bavaria, and this is one of the sketches that I did. Always keep your mind open for new experiences!

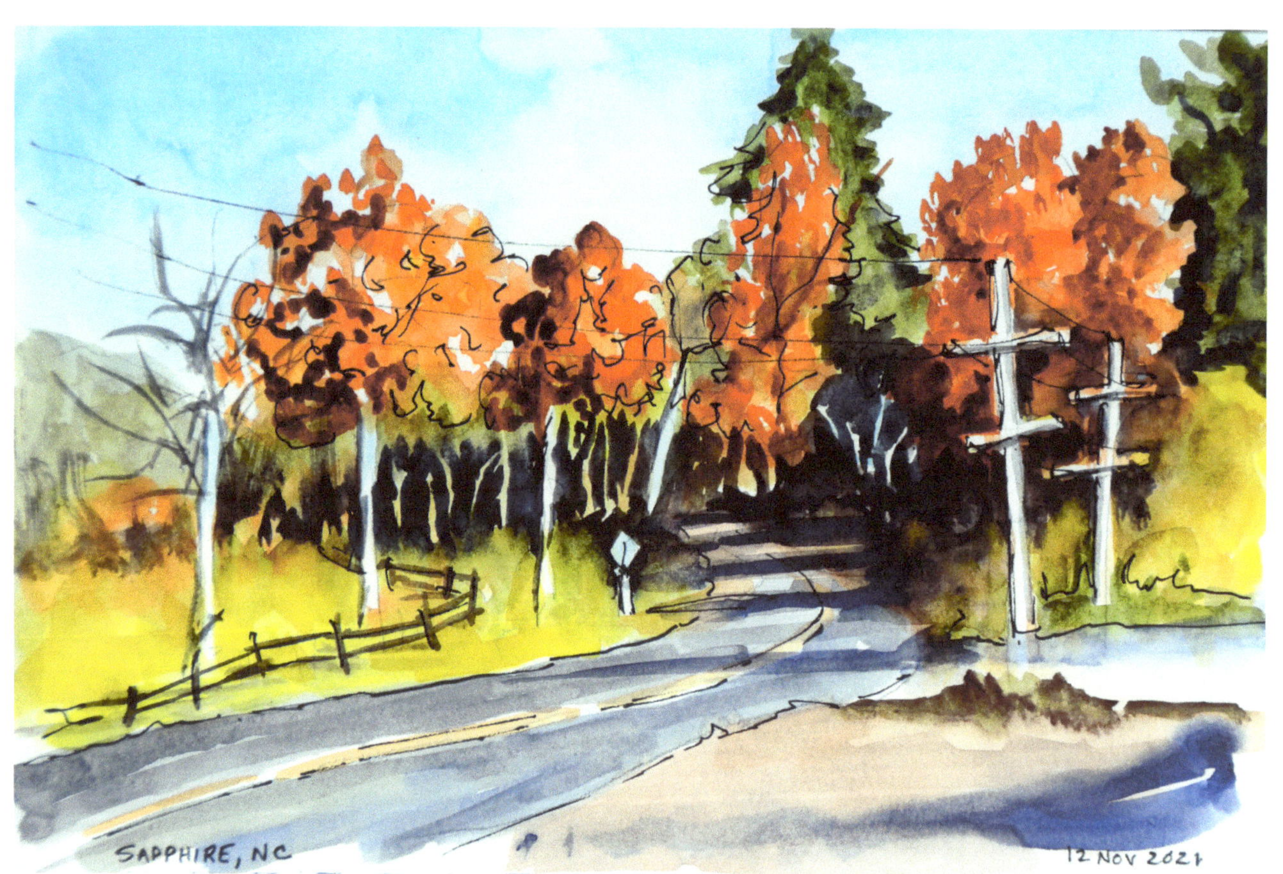

Sapphire Valley, NC
My wife and I were visiting some of her high school friends in Sapphire Valley, NC during the Fall when the leaves were changing colors. This is a great time to do sketches, so never pass up the opportunity to get outside and look for colorful views, even if it's a bit cold! This image was along one of the winding mountain roads that provided a pathway for the viewer's eye.

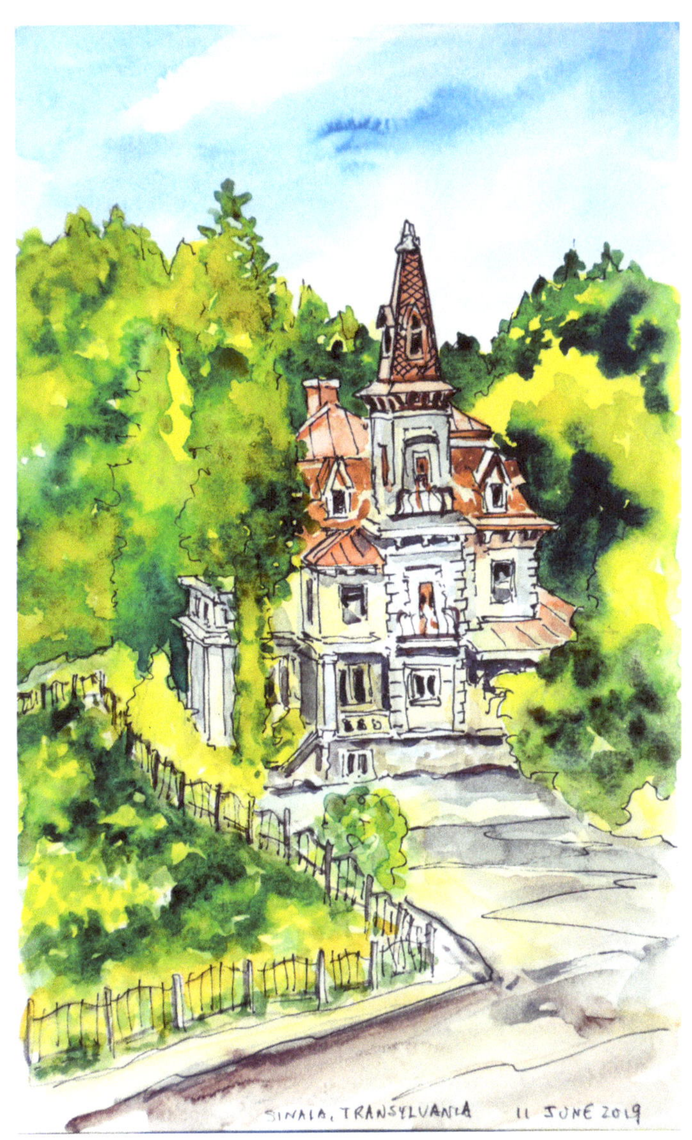

Transylvania

There were many scenes in Transylvania worthy of painting, but this sketch was right at my hotel balcony. You don't get this lucky very often, but be sure to look all around you wherever you go....you'll be surprised at what you may find. This old house looks like something right out of Mary Shelley's books.

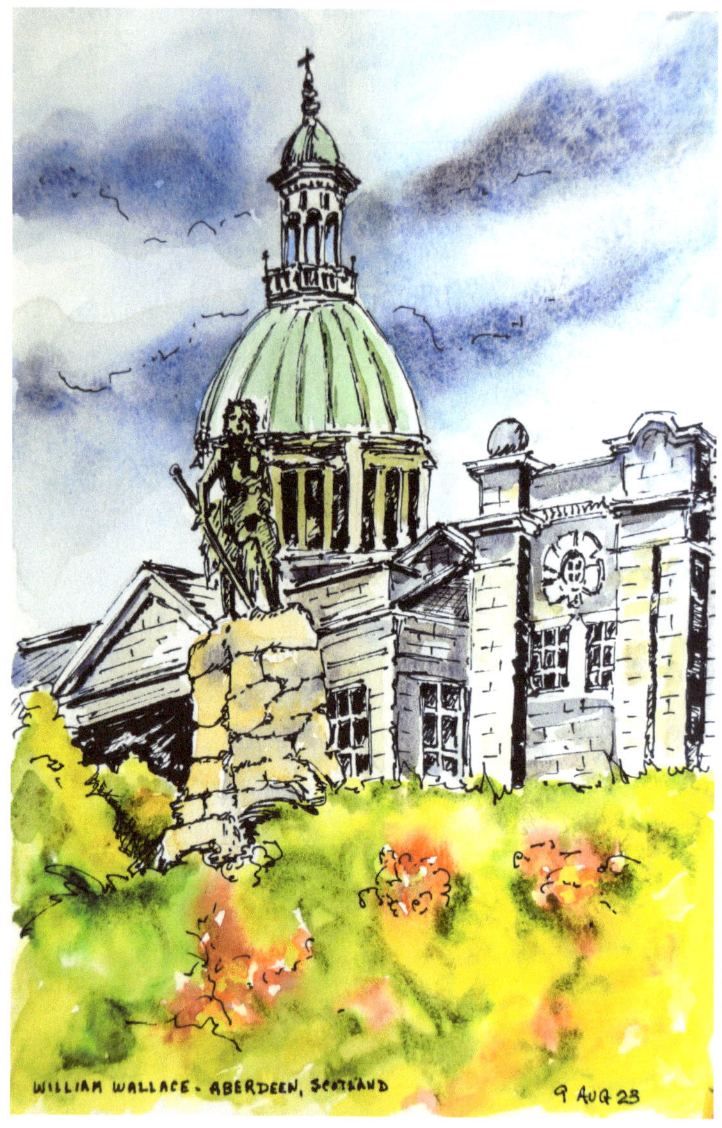

Aberdeen

On my Iceland trip, I missed my flight to Oslo, had my flight itinerary changed twice, and missed 2 days of the cruise! However, it worked to my advantage as the ship never made it's first scheduled port and then ran into a day of horrendous rough weather. The ship changed it's itinerary and went to Aberdeen, Scotland instead. I flew to Aberdeen ahead of the ship and met them there.   I had great weather in Aberdeen and did this sketch just 200 yards from my hotel! My luggage, unfortunately, didn't catch up with me for a couple of more days.

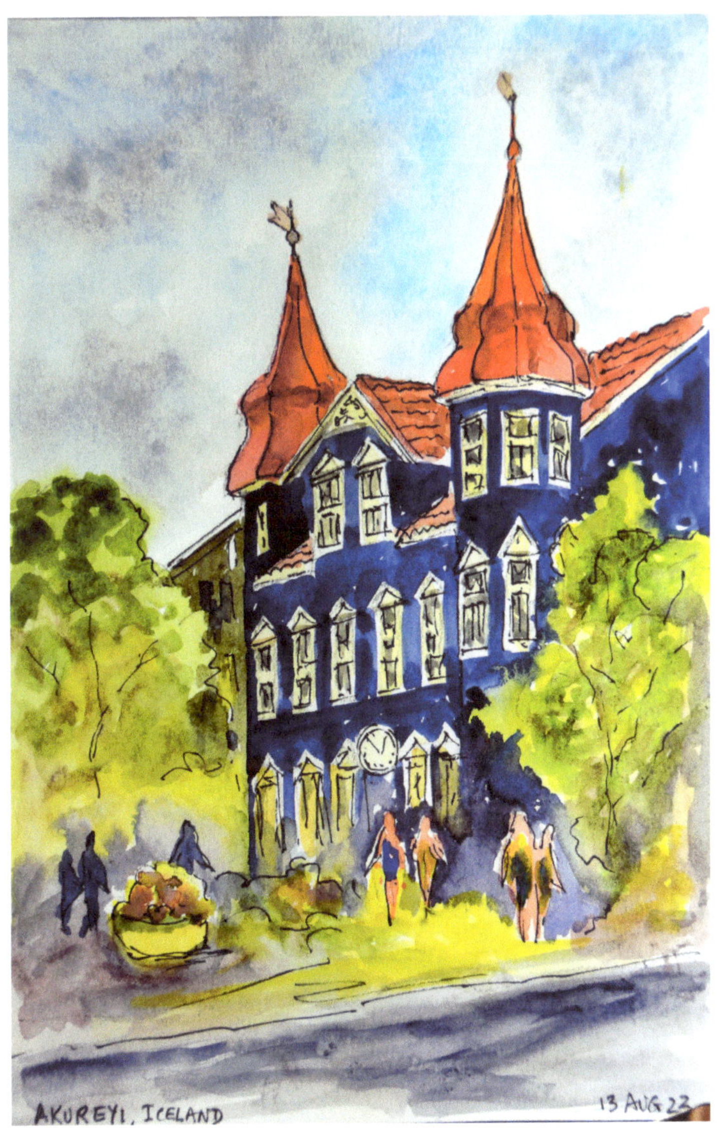

Akureyi

Akureyi, Iceland was our first stop in Iceland. It's a very scenic fishing port, not very large, but a place to take excursions out into the adjacent fjords and inland sites. I had free time for part of my day and went in to "old town" Akureyi, none of which is very old in Iceland. It was on a Sunday, and I was out on the streets before most people were up. This sketch was of a local hotel and cafe. Foot traffic picked up and I had many locals and some tourists stop by to watch and chat. In most places, the locals think I'm one of them until they hear the Southern accent and realize I'm American!

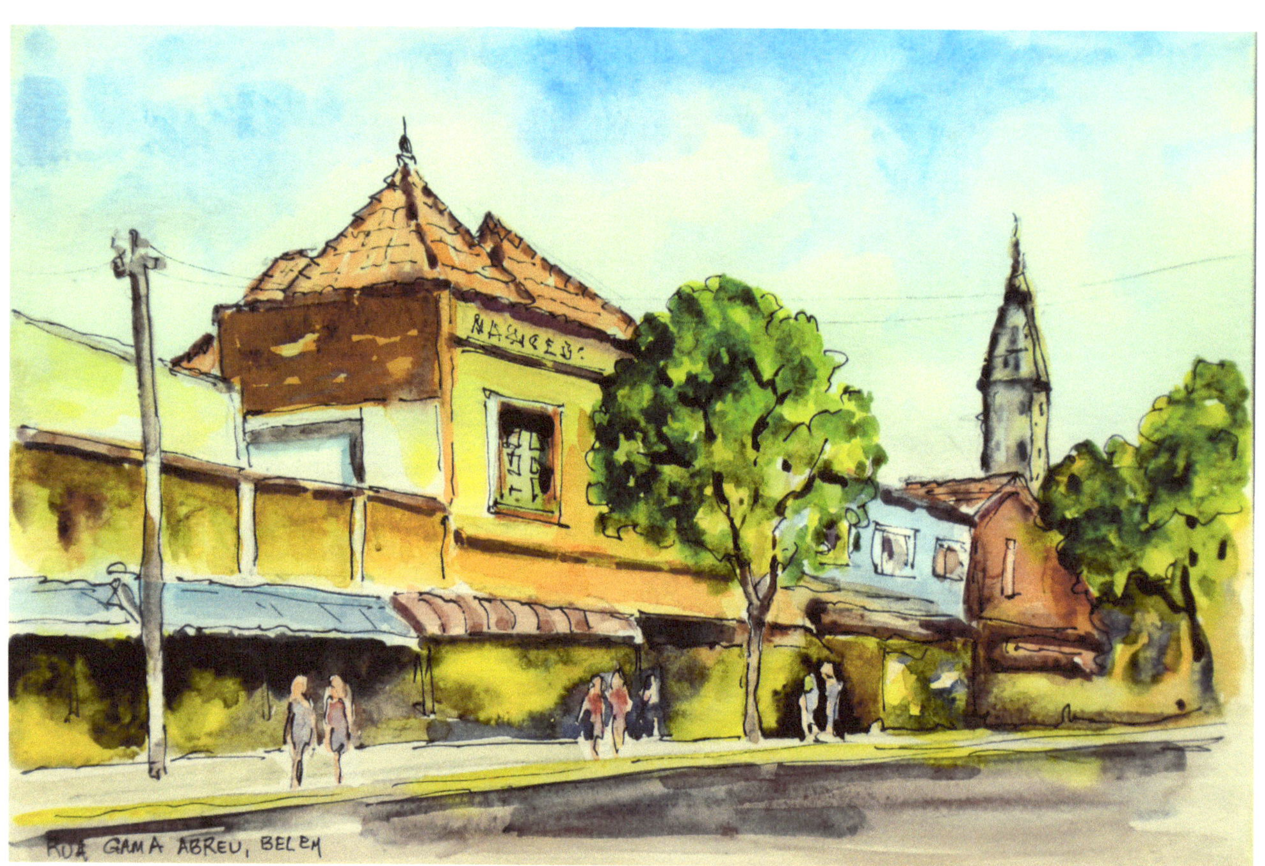

Belem, Brazil
Belem is a historical colonial city near the mouth of the Amazon river. My son and I were on the final leg of an Amazon trip that started near Manaus. This sketch is a view of one of the streets in the central section of town. When I found a spot to paint from, I realized that I'd forgotten my water bottle....rather than panic, I looked around and saw a tiny "convenience" store. I went in, found a bottle of water, and had to pay for it with a credit card. It cost about US 40 cents. You can always find a way to improvise when necessary!

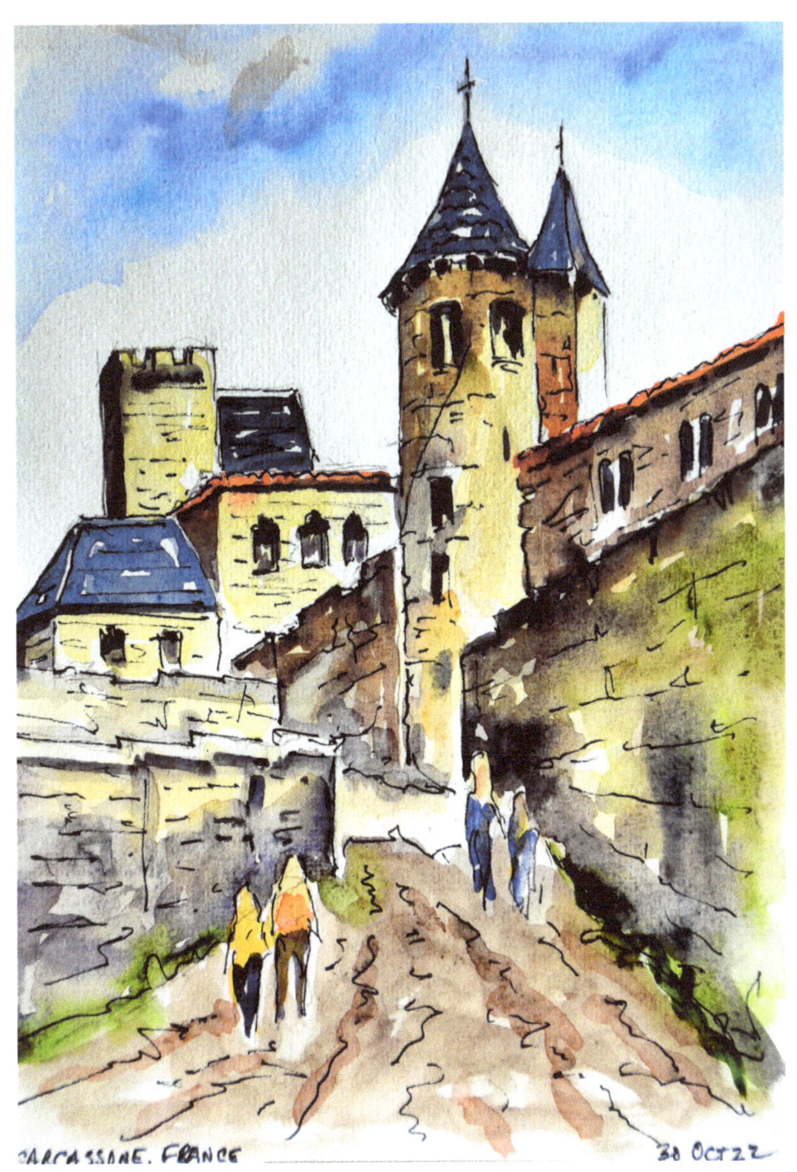

Carcassone, France
Carcassone is one the ancient walled medieval cities still standing in much of Europe. While there, I wandered the city taking pictures and doing sketches. This sketch was done on the outside of the wall going in to the back side of the city. Fortunately I had good lighting, but it was intermittently cloudy. I did a studio painting of a pair of Belgian draft horses from this outing.

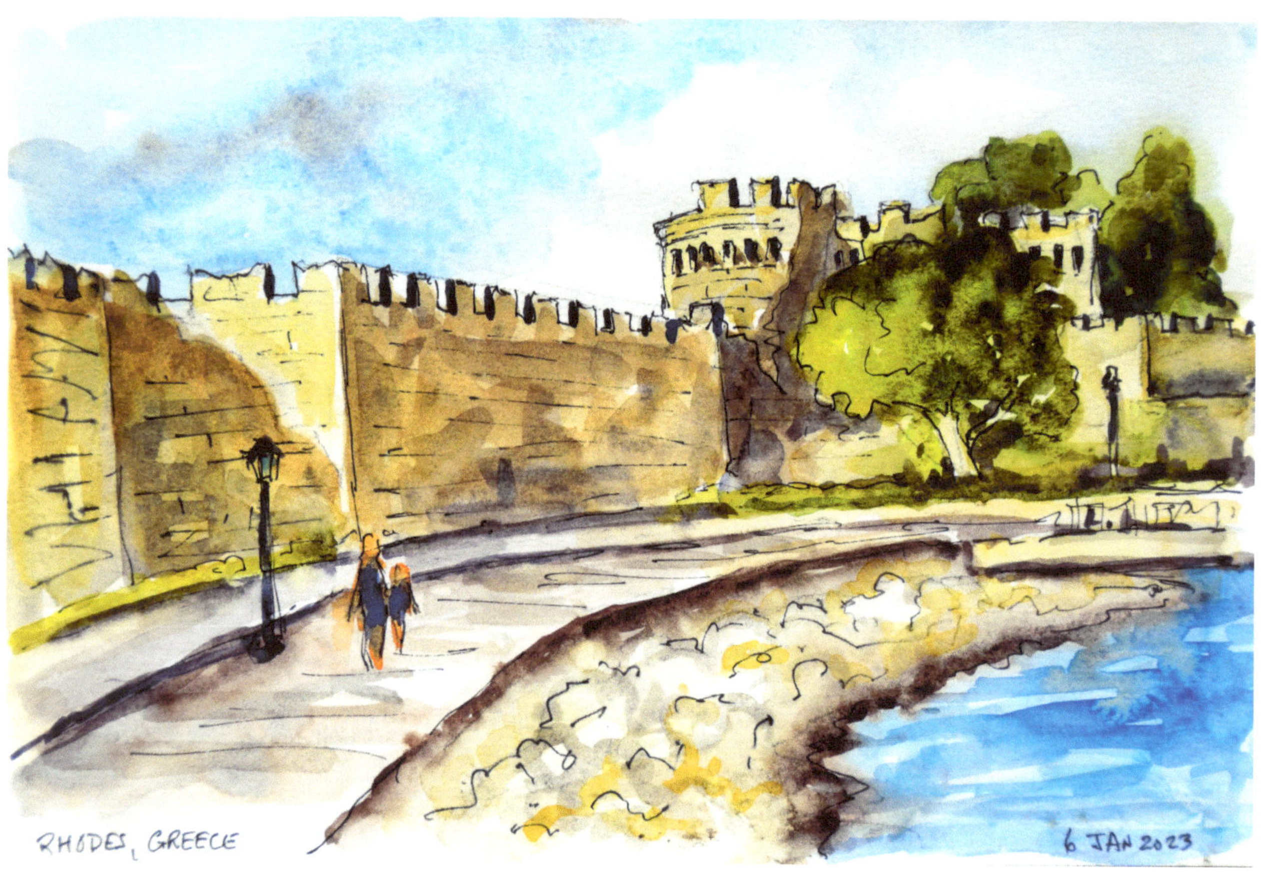

Crete

On a cruise from Athens to Istanbul, we stopped in Crete. The ship was only a 5 minute walk to the gates of the wall around the city. Inside the wall was interesting, but I liked the view from the harbor looking toward the outer wall of the city. I sat along the harbor walkway while doing this sketch and talked to quite a few interesting people as they passed by. As always, many of those were locals.

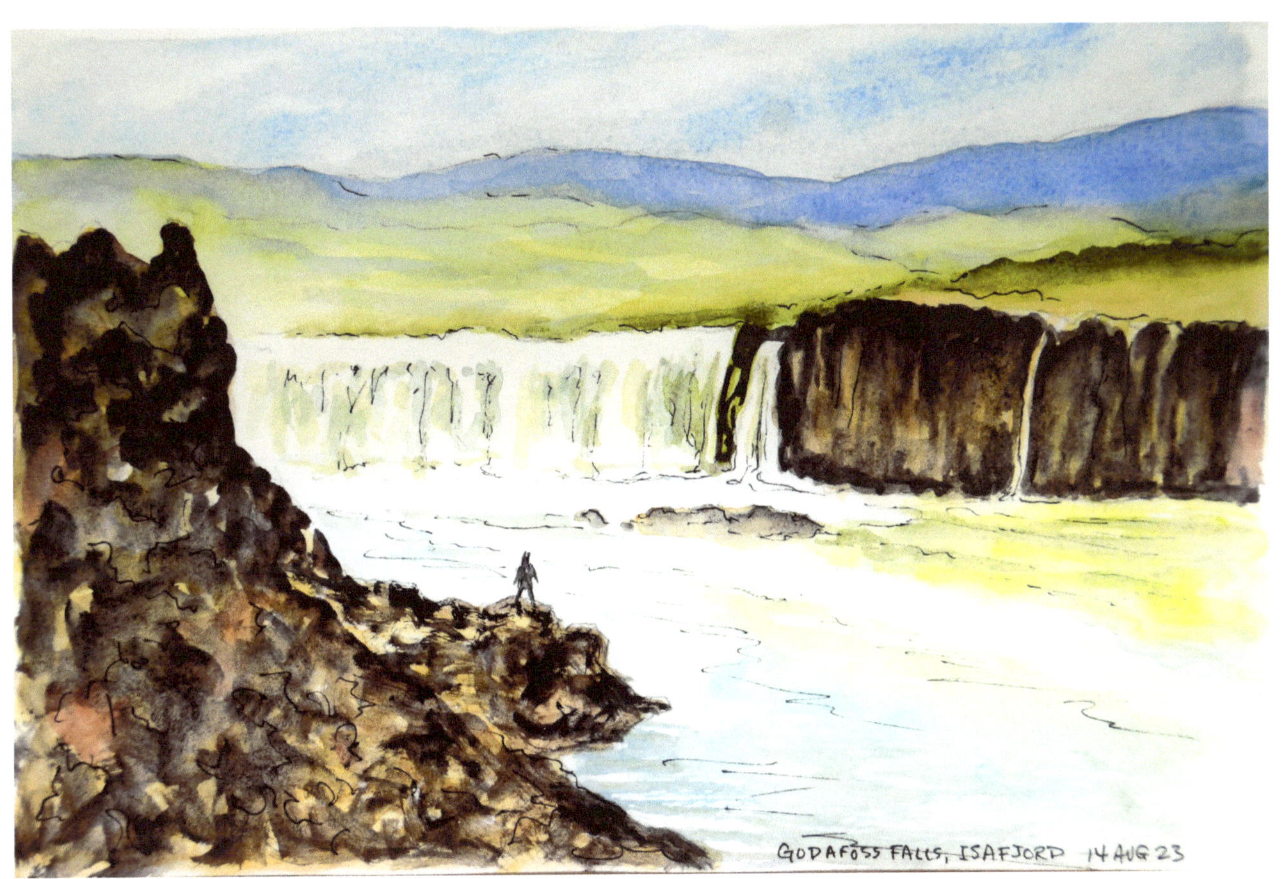

Godafoss Falls, Isafjord

Godafoss Falls is one of the most scenic waterfalls in Iceland (and, there are many). After about an hour long bus ride, we arrived at the parking area along the main road and walked about 300 yards to the cliffs overlooking the falls. The view from this sketch was done from the base of the cliffs, down almost at the river level. Surprisingly, there was not an extremely large crowd, so it was easy to explore all the views.   Painting the falls was relatively simple, as you just leave much of the paper white with a few glazes to partly subdue the pure white.

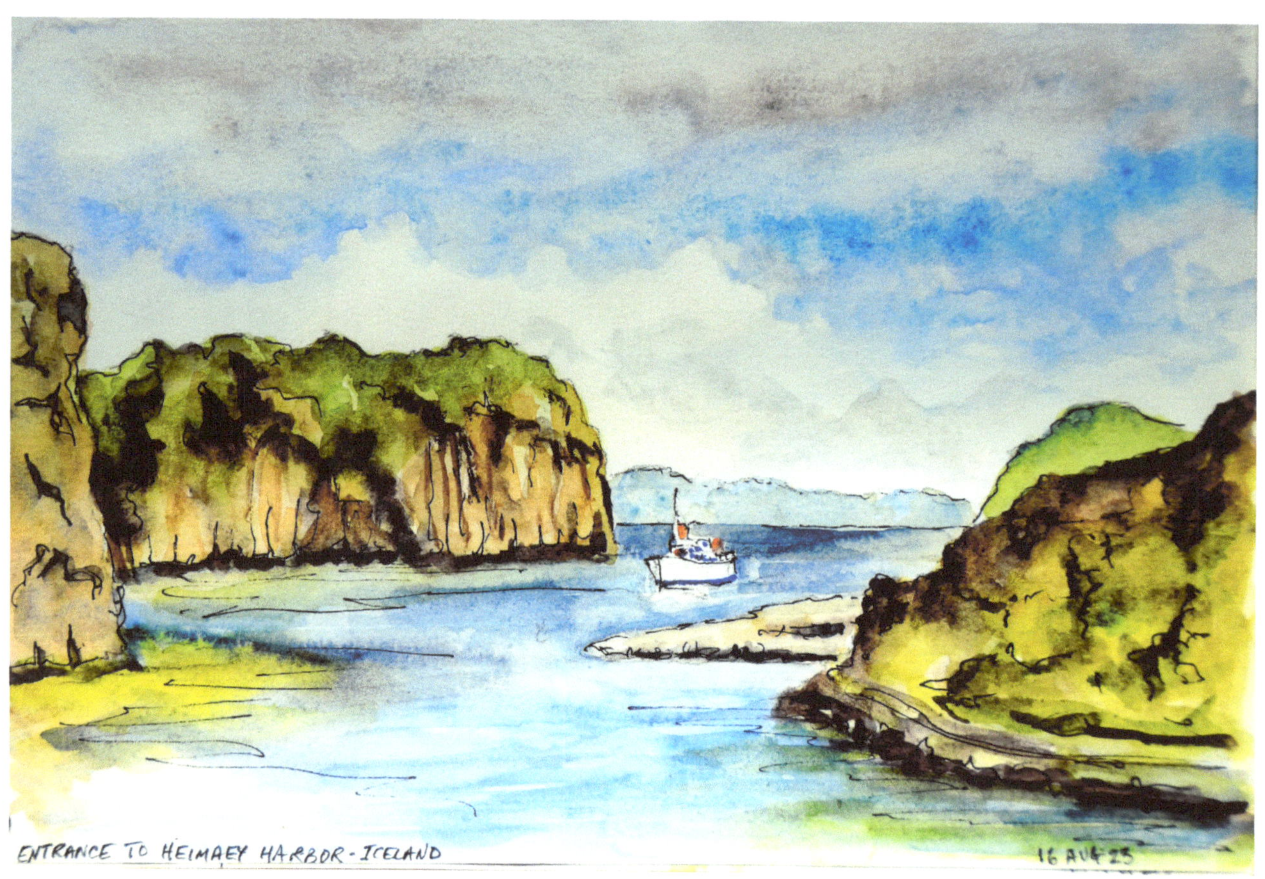

Heimaey Harbor

Heimaey is a small fishing port in a group of islands on the southwest part of Iceland. Our ship originally intended to anchor outside the harbor and tender passengers to the small port via the lifeboats. However, our captain decided he could maneuver through the narrow, twisting channel between the large cliffs. Somehow, he managed to do just that. This sketch shows that channel with the open sea in the distance.....and, with this sketch I'll never forget that brilliant feat!

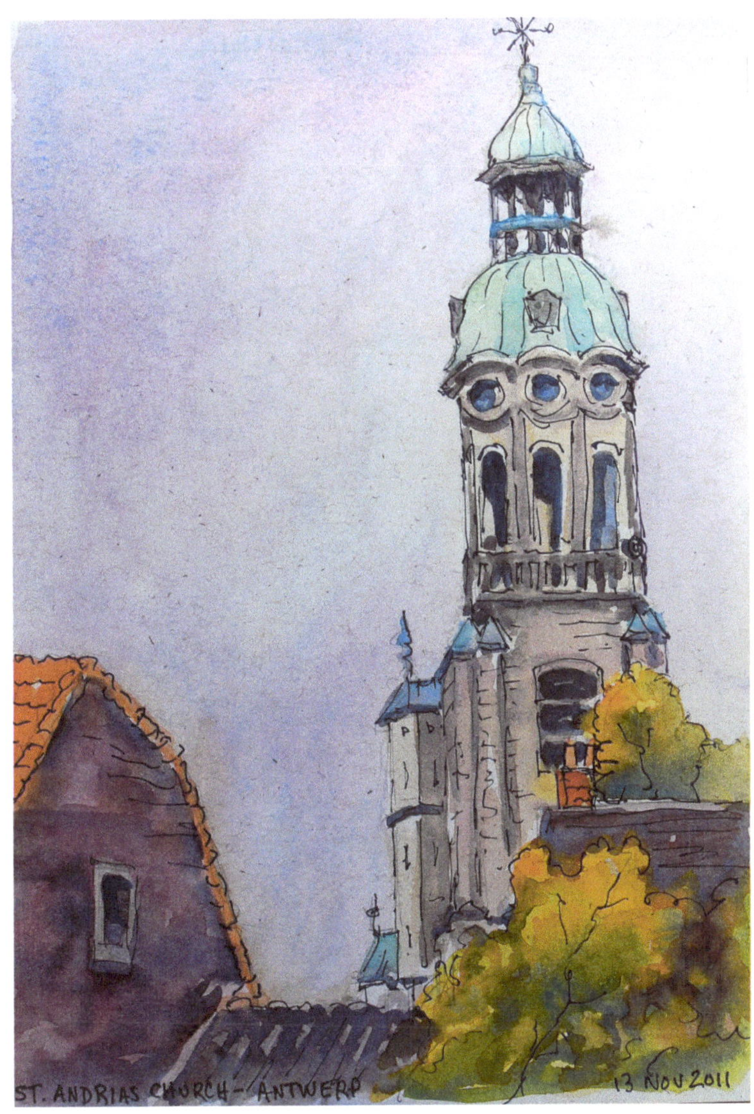

St Andrew's Church, Antwerp
St. Andrew's Church, Antwerp was another painting done on a cold, dreary day while our river boat was anchored in Antwerp. Louisa, once again, tagged along with a minimum of grumbling.   As we walked through Antwerp, we saw a church steeple in the distance, and that always leads me to a likely painting. Unfortunately, the temperature kept dropping rapidly and I encountered even harsher conditions later when I did the painting of St. Mary's Cathedral seen earlier in the book. That's when Louisa gave up and headed back to the boat to unthaw!

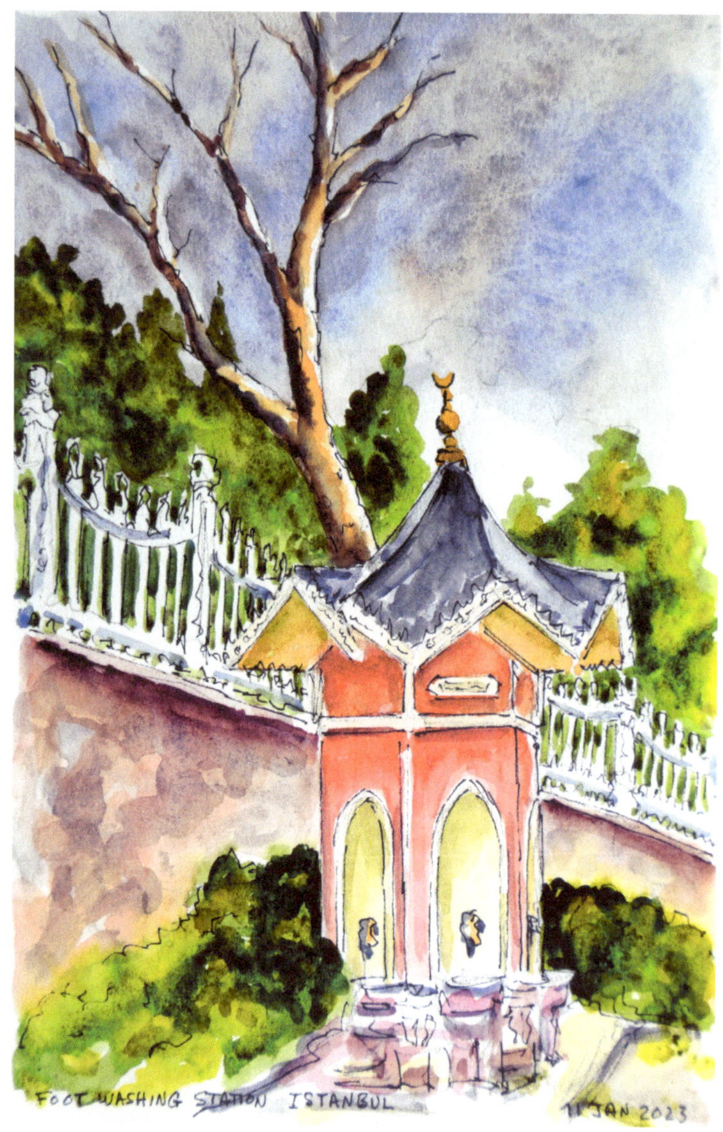

Istanbul
This sketch was done under less favorable conditions...I was in a hotel in Istanbul after debarking the ship and the weather had turned bad. Just down from the hotel was a small mosque which I did a sketch of just before the rain started. Behind the mosque, I found something even more artistic...a elaborate foot washing station just outside the mosque. Never overlook what seem mundane to you at the time!

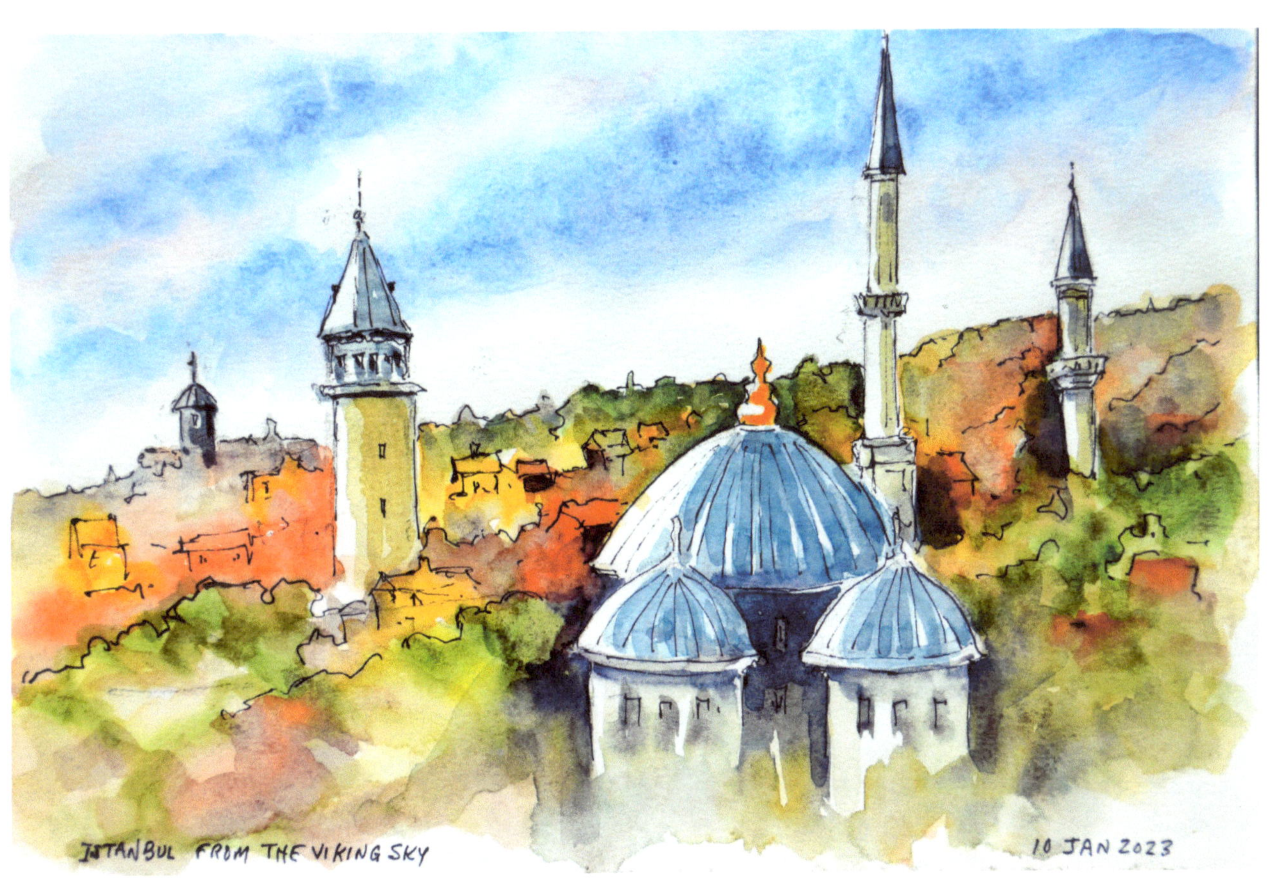

Istanbul
When you are with a group, you often don't have even a brief time to sketch, so you have to use what you have. In this case, there was a beautiful view of the modern side of Istanbul from the veranda on our ship. I comfortably sat in the shade with a cool drink and did this sketch. Sometimes you get lucky!

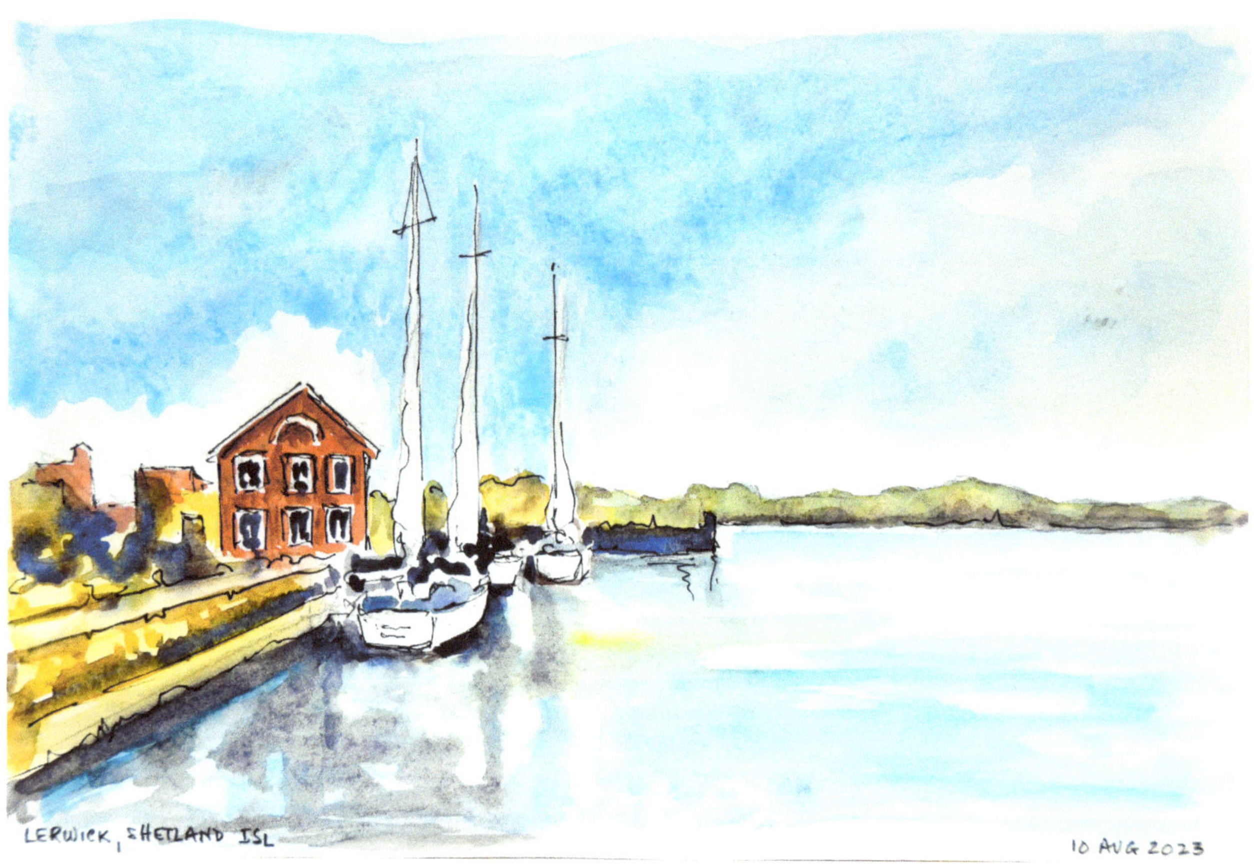

Lerwick, Shetland Islands

Lerwick, the main city in the Shetlands, was a quaint port city with an interesting history.   A group of us walked most of the entire old city including Fort Charlotte. The most historic buildings were along the downtown waterfront and there were only smaller fishing boats and sailboats in this area. With time being short, I picked a wharf scene with sailboats, but left some of them out of the painting. Many times, you have to simplify because of time constraints and to improve the composition!

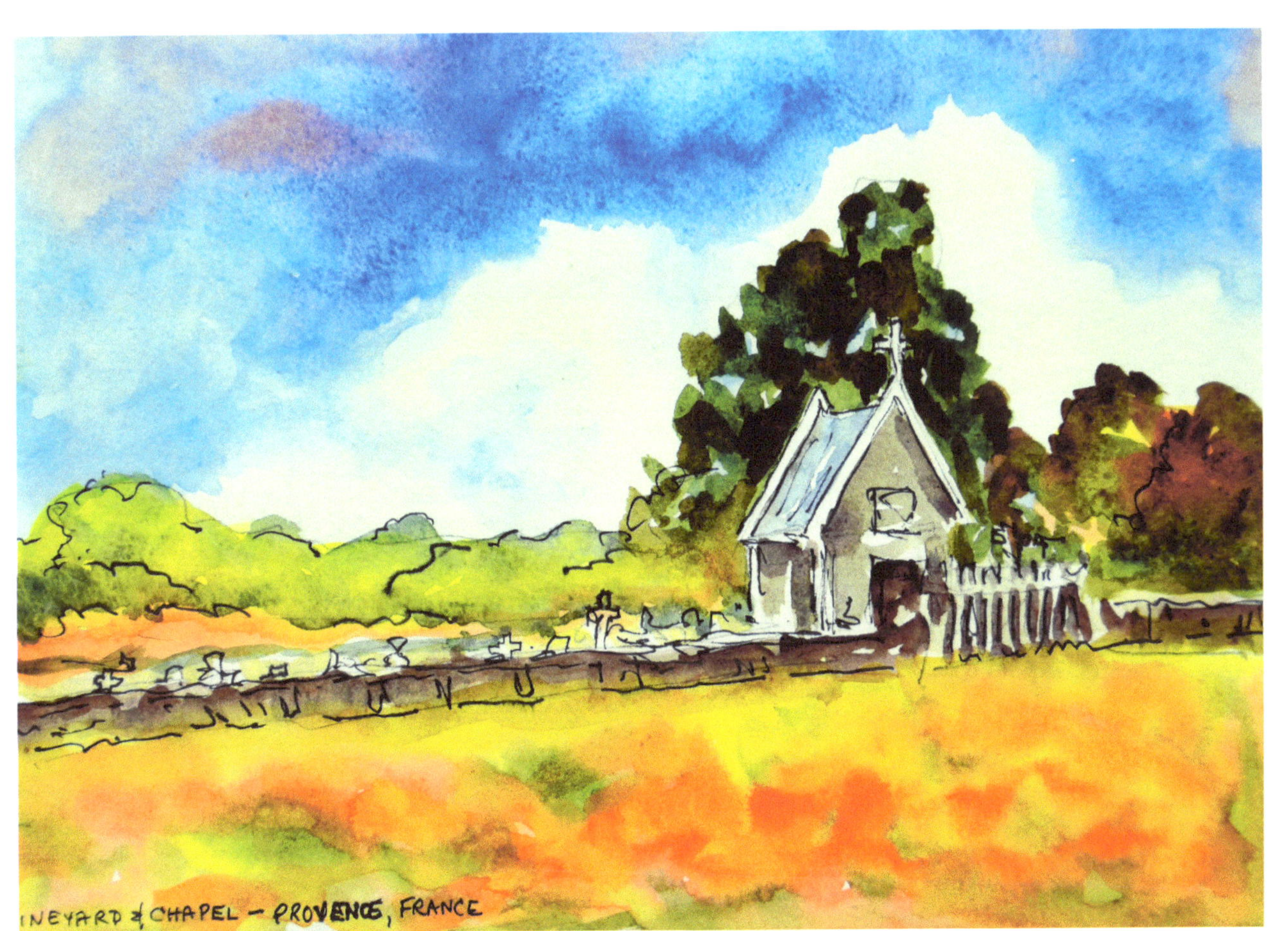

Provence, France
While on a tour to a vineyard in Provence, we had some free time to wander about the premises. This sketch portrays the vineyard,
but the building in the middle ground is a small chapel with a cemetery surrounding the chapel. What a wonderful scenic background
to honor your ancestors.

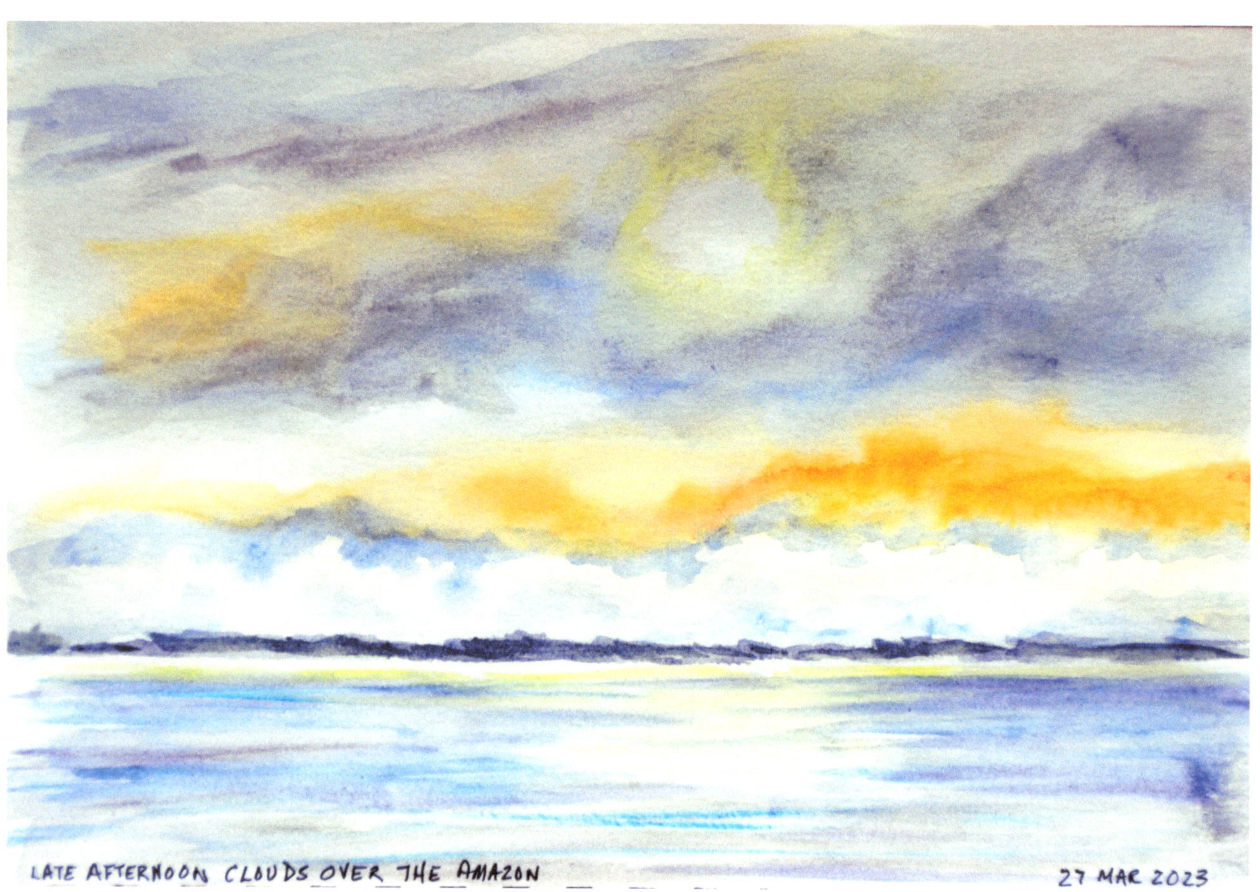

Amazon Clouds
While cruising upstream on the widest part of the Amazon, we saw some gorgeous late afternoon clouds. I don't usually do scenes with just sky and water, but this appealed to me. Again, a reminder that you need to always look around you....scenes will appear to you!

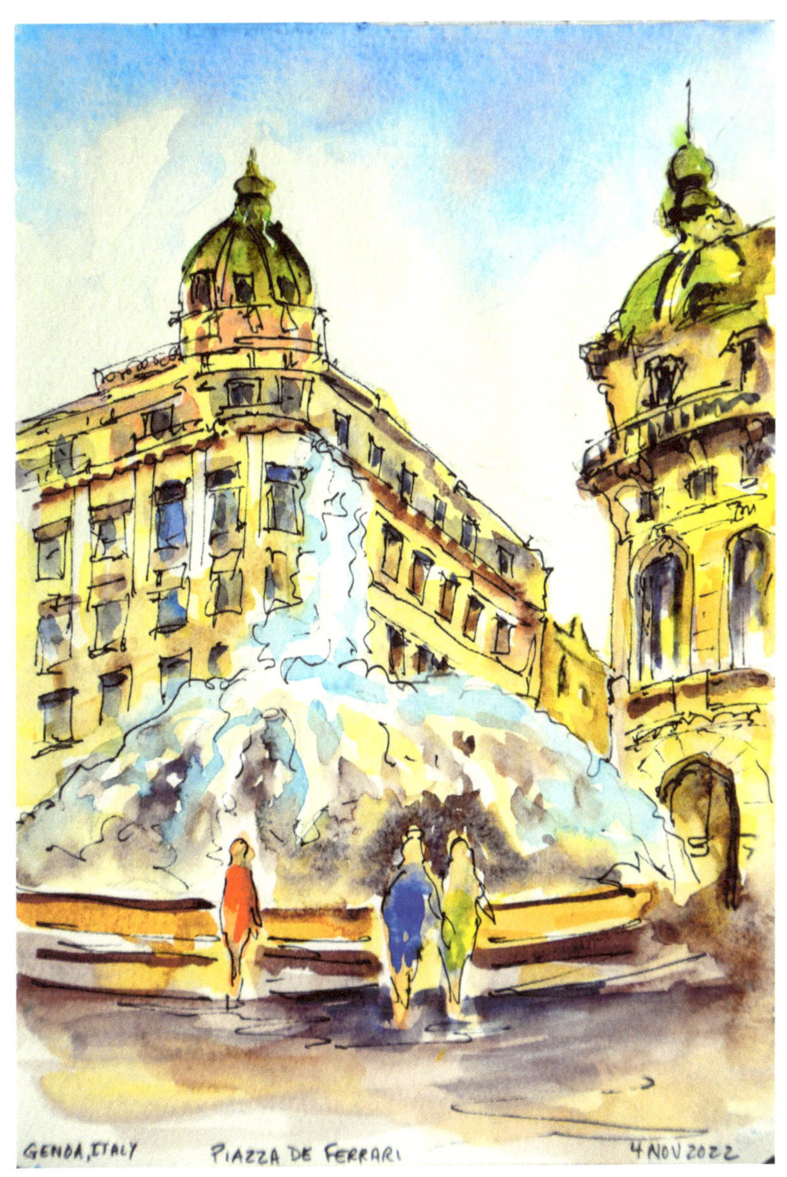

Genoa

Our ship was supposed to go on to Corsica from Nice, but there was torrential rain and rough seas around Corsica, so the captain made a decision to go to Genoa, Italy instead. It turned out to be a wise decision as Genoa had beautiful, sunny weather the whole time we were there and the city had so much to offer. This sketch is of the water fountain in one of the central squares of Genoa.

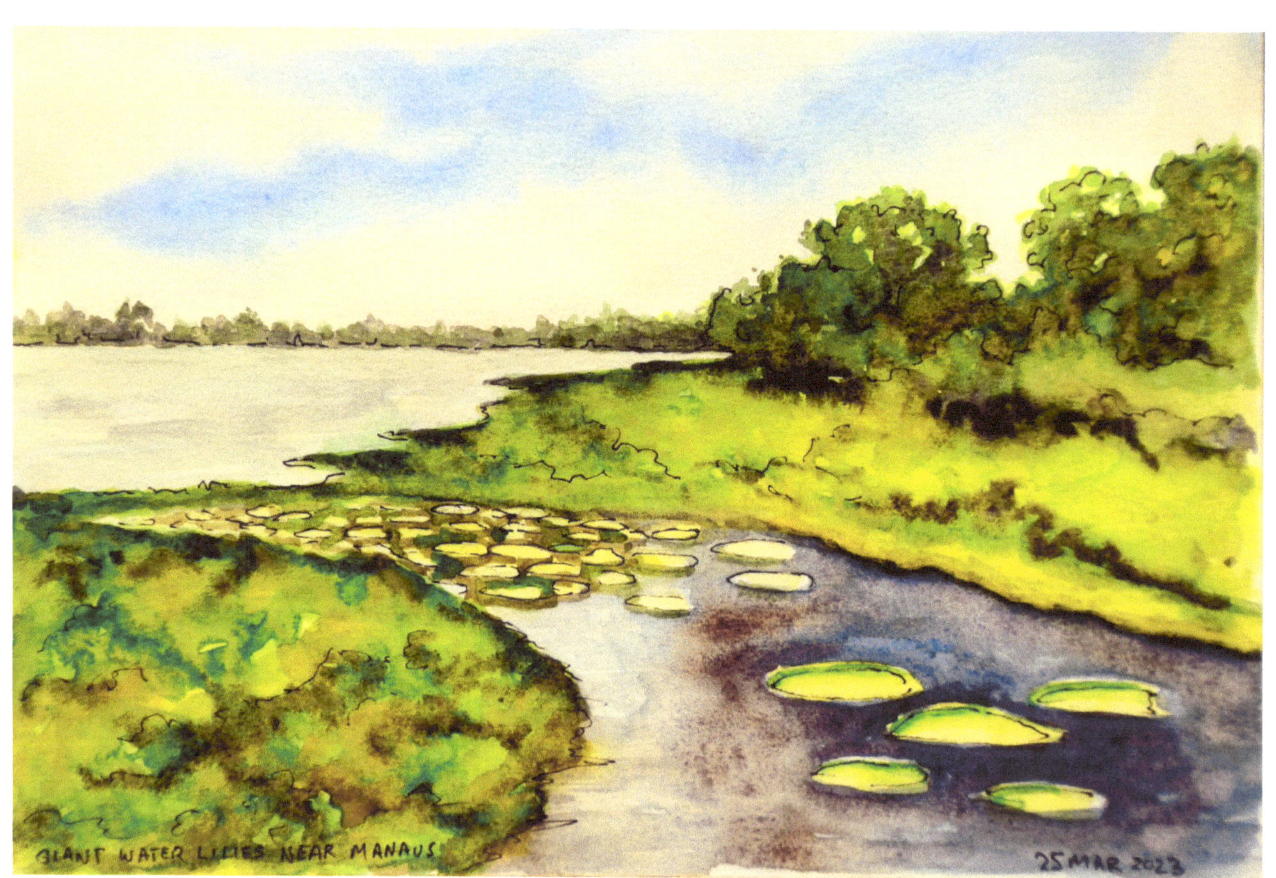

Giant Lilies

On my Amazon trip, most of our excursions were done on inflatable Zodiacs. This sketch was done of the giant water lilies just northeast of Manaus. To get there, we went through a downpour of rain on the Zodiacs. We all looked like drowned rats by the time we got back. I had do this sketch from the comfort of the ship. Don't be afraid of the weather....it's part of plein air sketching!

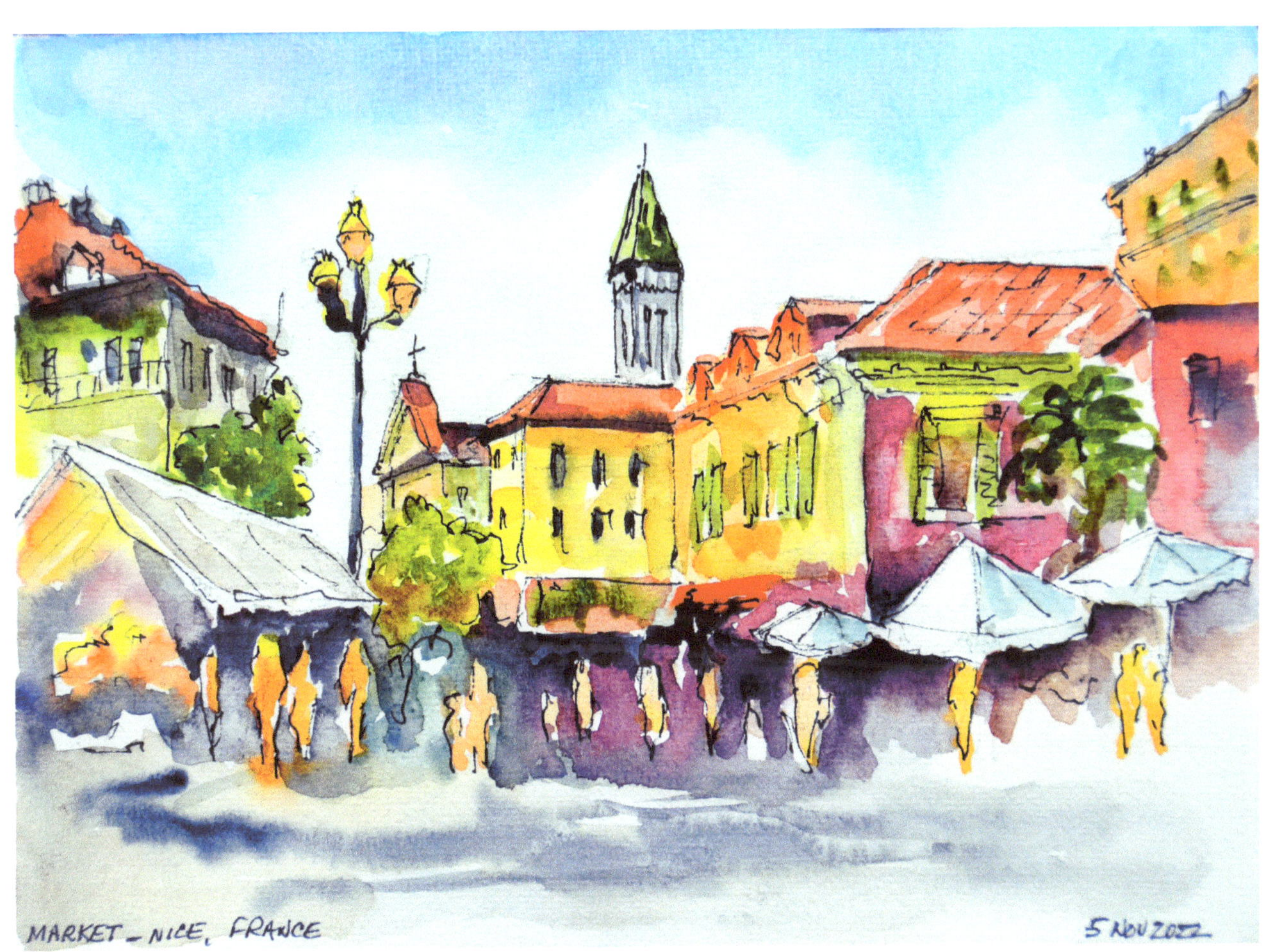

Nice Market

I spent an extra overnight stay in Nice after having been there a few days before, so I had a chance to scope out what I wanted to paint. Old town Nice is very picturesque, but one of the most fascinating parts was the market. It was busy and active with mostly locals. There were a lot of great views, but few with a place you could paint from due to the pedestrians! In this case, I found a nice view from the outside tables of a cafe. There I sat down, ordered a coffee and pastry, and worked from my table. My waitress was curiously watching and gave me a thumbs up when I finished. Most cafes love to have you order something and attract folks passing by. I finished in less time than the French usually take to finish their coffee!

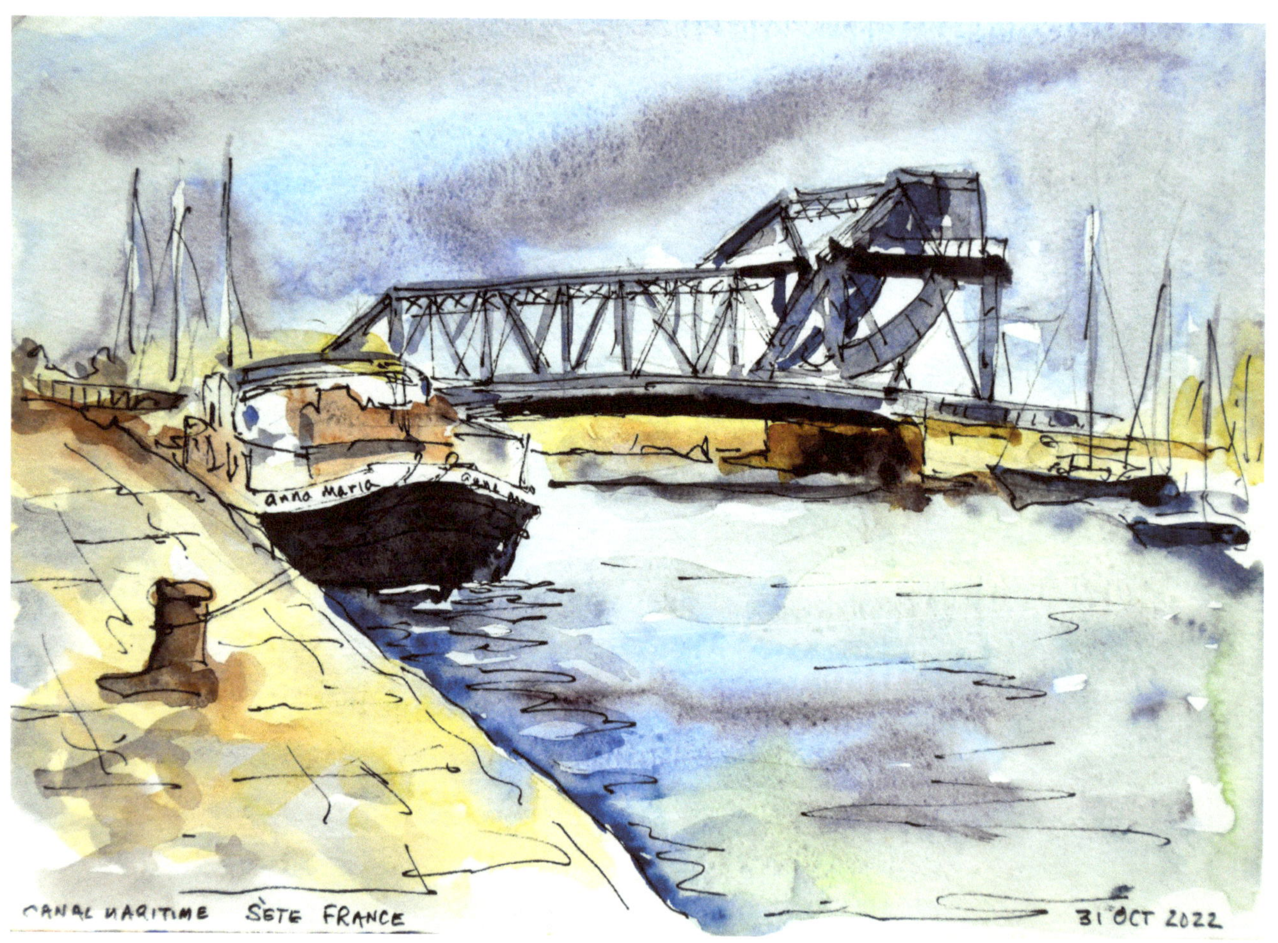# Sete, France

Sete is sometimes known as the Venice of France, although I think Strasbourg's canals were more scenic. I had a day on my own to wander the canals through out the city and did several sketches. It stayed overcast and threatened to rain the whole time, but I was lucky. It's a good idea to have lightweight raingear just in case. This sketch is along one of the quays in Sete.

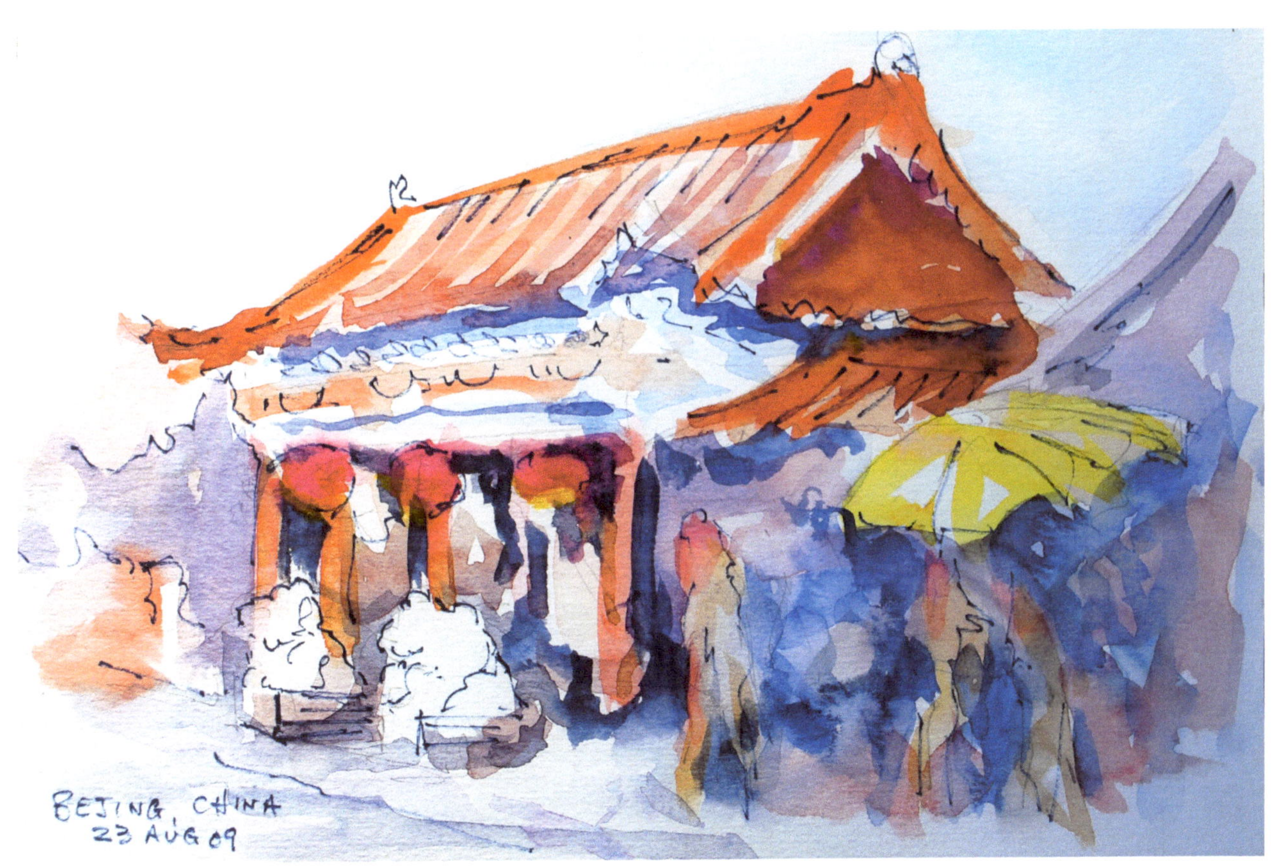

Beijing

This sketch in Beijing was one of my quickest...about 15 minutes! We were with a group staying in the old Majestic Hotel downtown and everyone else headed back while I decided that I had to paint this typical old Chinese architecture. I didn't have much time, so it had to be quick. The two items in the left foreground are seated lion statues...you have to use your imagination to see those, but the shapes worked well as negative images.

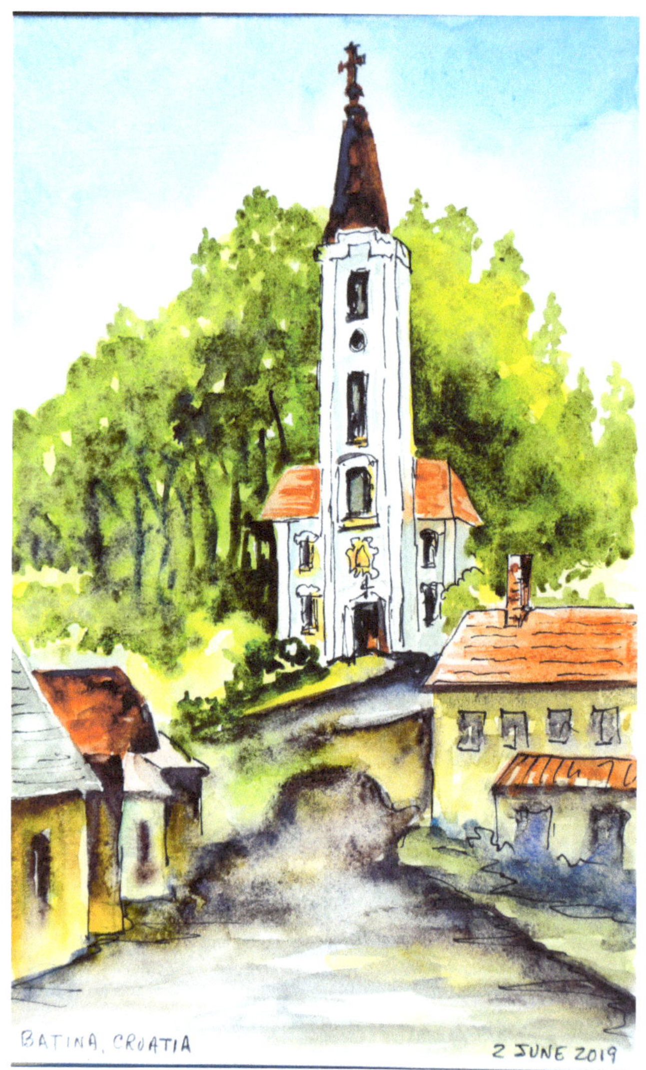

Batina, Croatia

This view from Batina, Croatia exemplifies the ease with which we may find a sketch. The riverboat was anchored early in the morning and before breakfast, I went to the upper deck and found this view. Church steeples always make a good subject especially when you can paint them as negative shapes surrounded by a darker background. Here we framed the white tall tower by the darker trees and the dark steeple by the lighter skies. That morning, I had a chair and table that I could arrange for the best angle and sit in comfort with a cup of hot coffee. Only the crew was up this early and I had conversations with them as I painted. Some artists dislike being interrupted by bystanders, but I find it to be part of the experience.

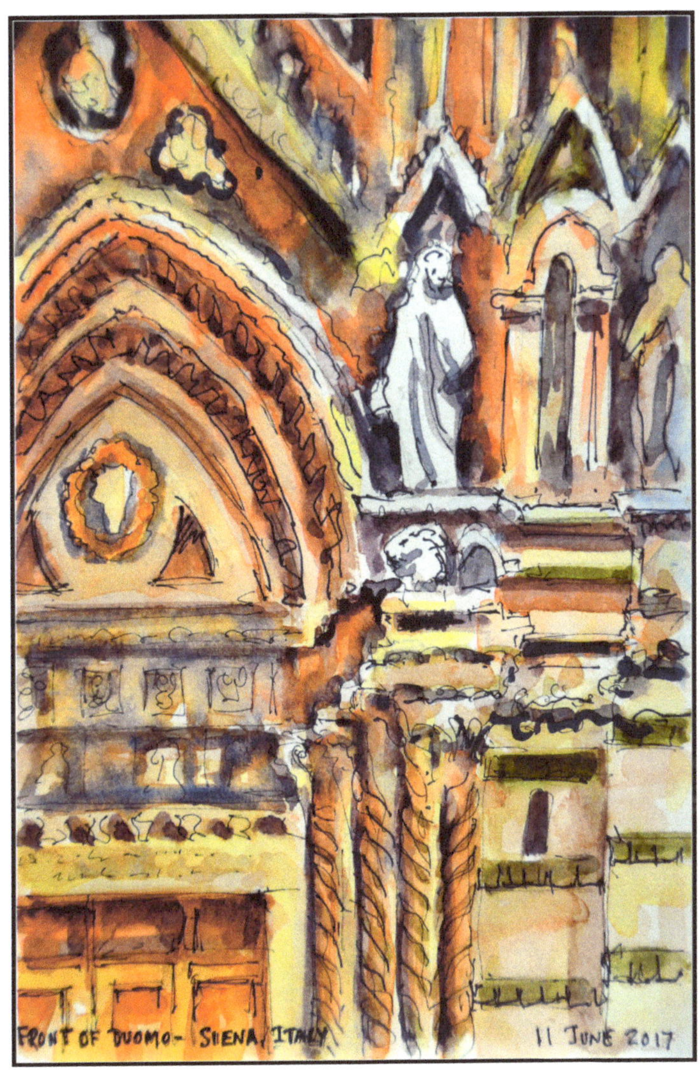

Duomo, Siena

We had a magnificent trip to Italy where we stayed several days outside Siena in a gorgeous setting with olive and fruit trees overlooking a beautiful landscape. I did several paintings around where we stayed, but we also went into the Old Town of Siena and found many subjects to paint there as well. A short walk from the main square, I found the Duomo with a smaller square around it. What intrigued me most was the elaborate and colorful exterior of the Duomo with sculptures of religious figures, various animals and other beasts! I don't usually try to do this type of journal painting, but I had to try. It did take longer than most!

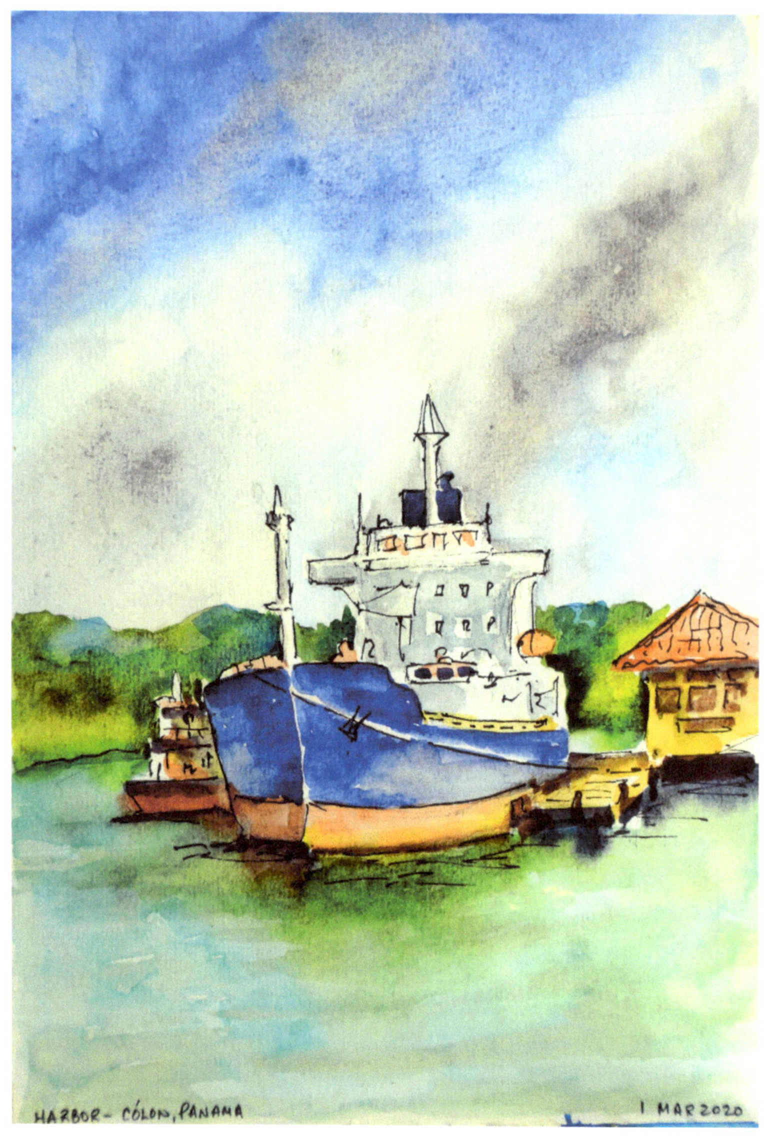

Colon Panama

The port of Colon, Panama is a short distance from the Caribbean entrance to the Panama Canal. As you can guess, it's a tremendously busy port with some ships transferring cargo to other ships to go through the canal and others picking up or unloading goods from the port itself. Most of the scenic spots are on on the water in some shape or form. Here again, looking for interesting shapes is key to creating a successful sketch. In this painting, note how all parts of the painting are overlapped and linked together.

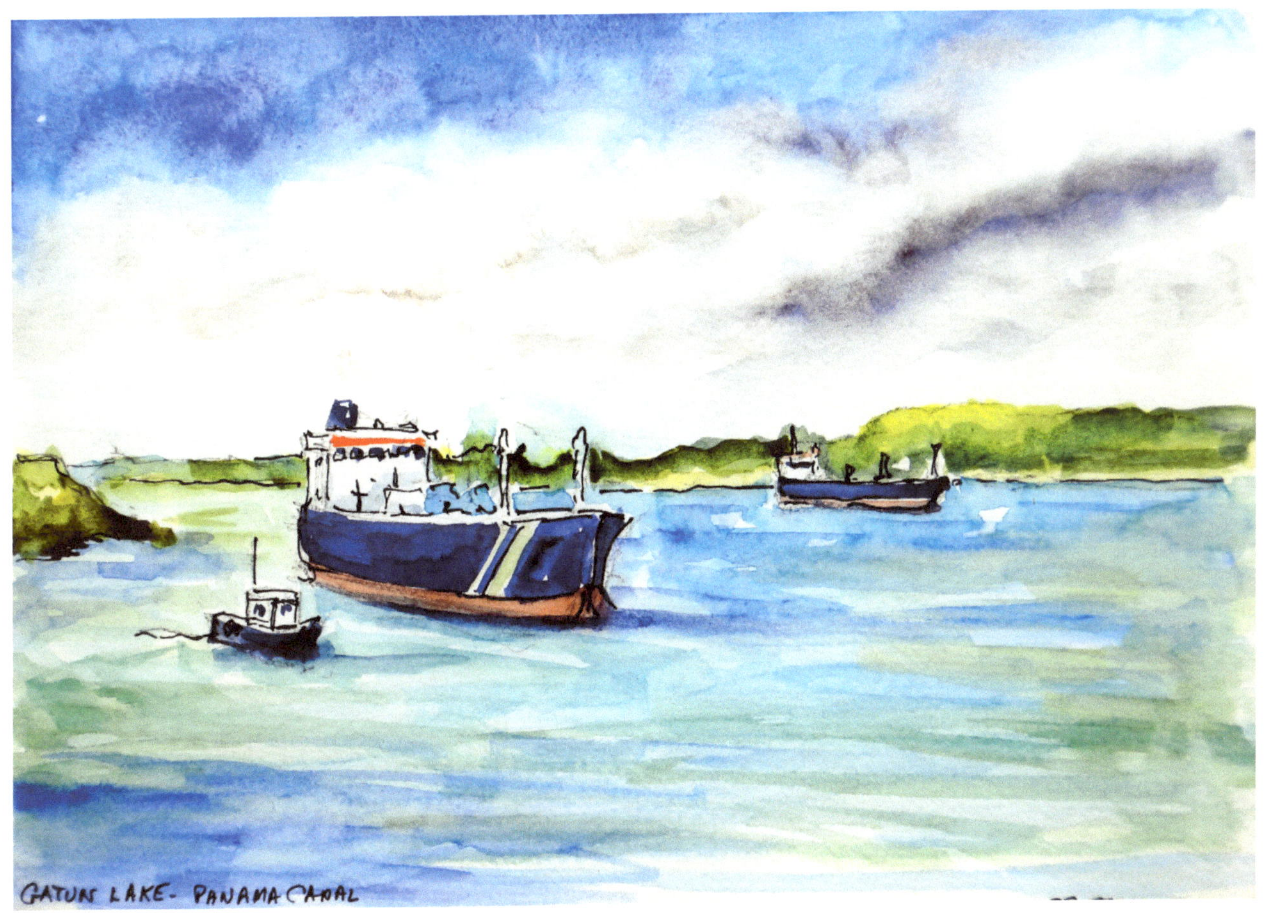

Gatun Lake, Panama Canal
The Panama Canal is one of the marvels of the world and much of the old technology is still functioning. This sketch shows Gatun Lake where ships congregate waiting to head through the locks to the Atlantic or Pacific side. At times there are quite a few ships in line, so you have a lot of views to choose from. Look for good side lighting where the ships cast shadows and make sure you interlock/overlap the ships with the distant background. Move them if necessary.

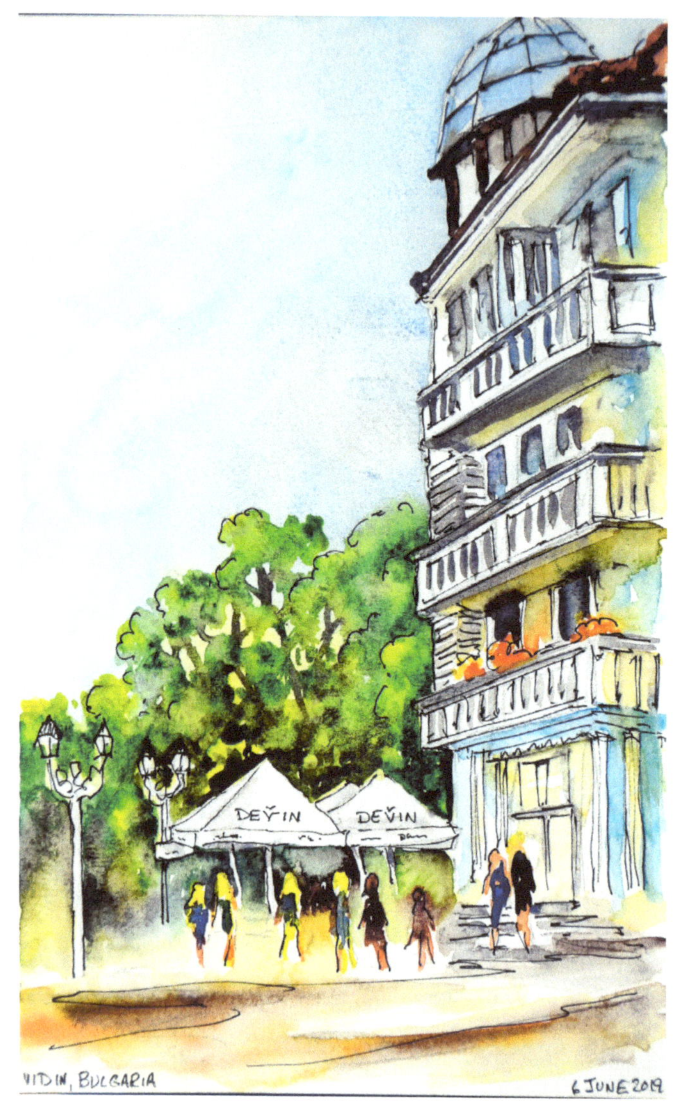

Vidin, Bulgaria

Once again, many great sketches can be found right away.   This view from Vidin, Bulgaria is one of those. The riverboat was moored only about 150 feet from where I did this painting. This brings me to emphasize that river boats are an excellent way to travel regarding ease of finding places to sketch. They almost always anchor right in the middle of the historic sections of riverfront towns, and you can easily walk into the town center, and get back to the boat easily if needed.

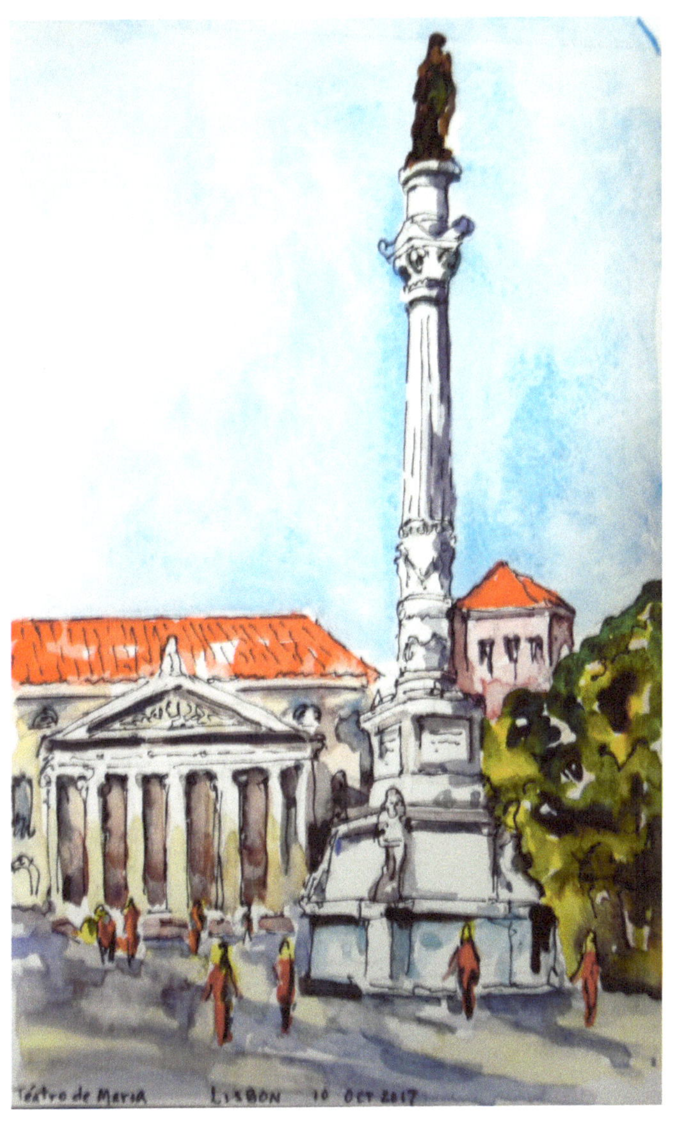

Teatro de Maria

Lisbon was also one of my favorite places to visit and paint as well as to take photographs. Teatro de Maria was a large theater on one side of the main square and this area was teeming with people beginning every morning. I did many portrait/figure studio paintings from the photos I took with a telephoto lens. I think this square had more interesting people than I have ever seen in an area that size! Near the theater was Lisbon's Wall of Tolerance, with "tolerance" spelled in many languages. On benches below this wall sat a very diversified group of people...as if they were physically attracted to this wall!

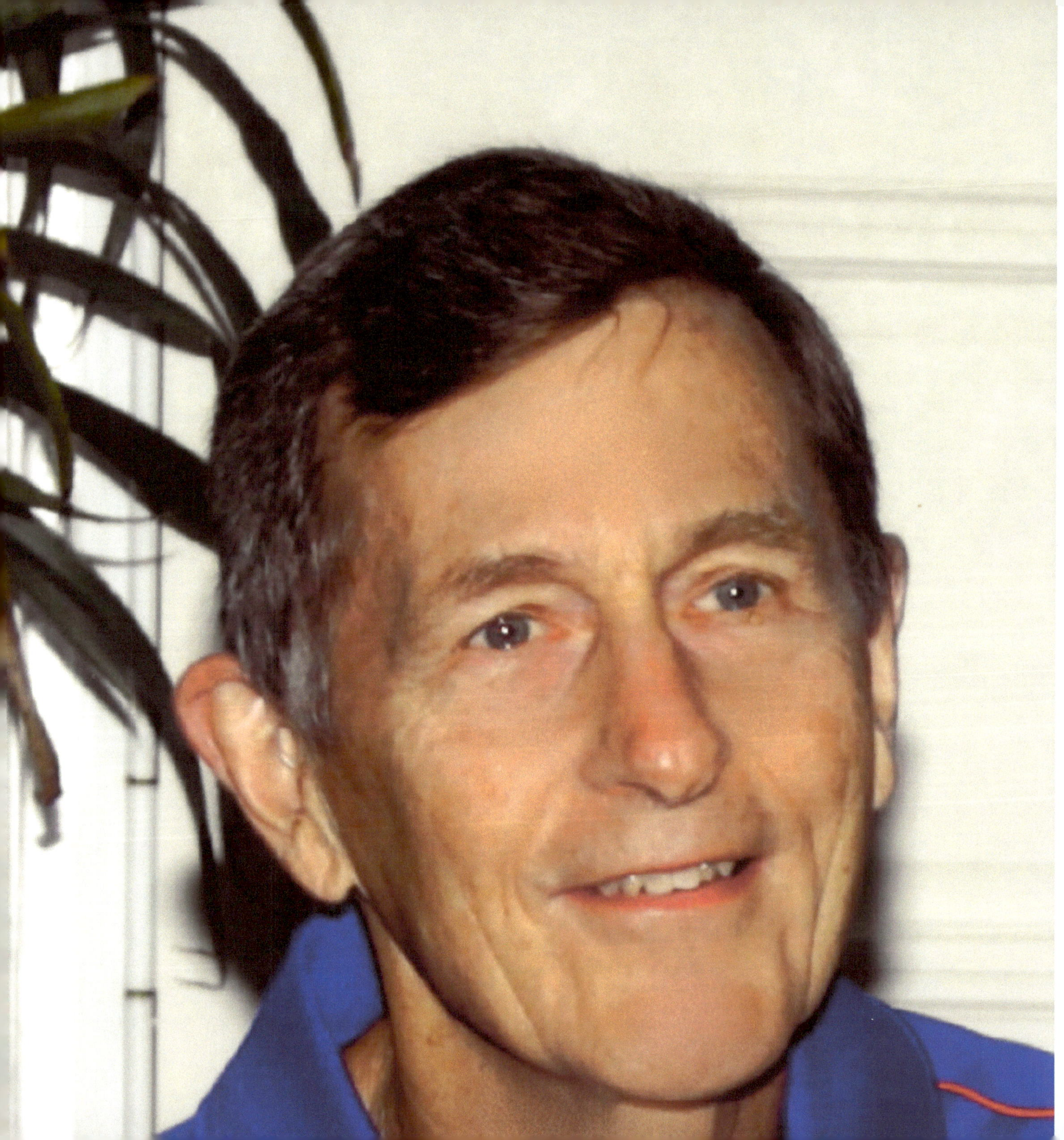

DON TAYLOR

PLEIN AIR JOURNALING IN WATERCOLOR AND PEN & INK

Published by the Contemporary Art Station.
All artworks © 2024 Don Taylor "Plein Air Journaling in Watercolor and Pen & Ink"

ISBN: 978-84-19926-85-2
DL: GR 9-2024

Printed in Europe by Contemporary Art Station.

DON TAYLOR

PLEIN AIR JOURNALING IN WATERCOLOR AND PEN & INK